Read This, Save Lives

---

*A TEACHER'S GUIDE TO CREATING SAFER
CLASSROOMS FOR LGBTQ+ STUDENTS*

Read This, Save Lives

A TEACHER'S GUIDE TO CREATING SAFER CLASSROOMS FOR LGBTQ+ STUDENTS

By Sameer Jha

Read This, Save Lives—first edition, September 2018.

ISBN: 9781720196976

Visit us online at www.theempathyalliance.org and subscribe to receive bonus materials and videos.

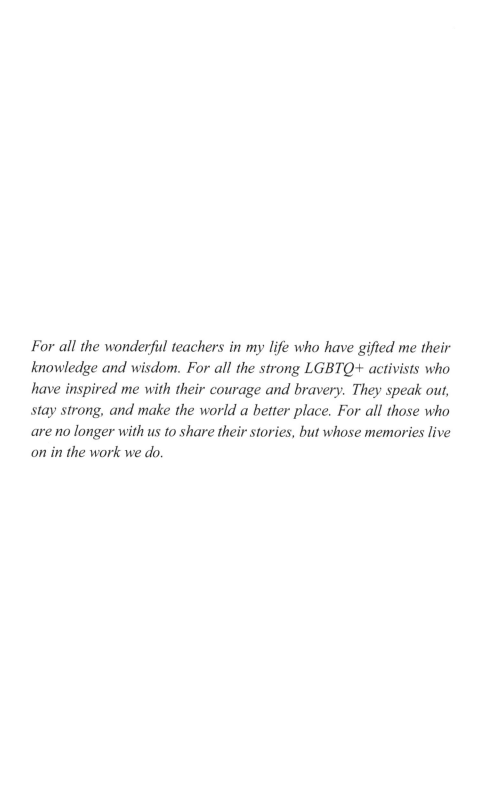

For all the wonderful teachers in my life who have gifted me their knowledge and wisdom. For all the strong LGBTQ+ activists who have inspired me with their courage and bravery. They speak out, stay strong, and make the world a better place. For all those who are no longer with us to share their stories, but whose memories live on in the work we do.

Table of Contents

Author's Note	xi
Chapter One: WHY THIS BOOK MATTERS	1
The Extent Of Bullying In Schools	2
Sobering Statistics	3
You Are Teaching LGBTQ+ Students	5
"Gay" Should Not Be A Slur	6
What I Have Learned About Bullying	8
Chapter Two: PUTTING AN END TO ANTI-LGBTQ+ SLURS	12
You Are Not Alone In This Journey	13
Interrupt + Educate Every Time You Hear Anti-LGBTQ+ Insults	15
STEP 1: Interrupt	*16*
STEP 2: Educate	*17*
Beyond "So Gay": When Bullying Escalates	20
Never Ignore Complaints	*23*
Listen and Protect	*23*
Report the Bullying	*24*
Seek Professional Help	*24*
Prevention: Stop Bullying Before It Starts	25
The Ripple Effect	26
Chapter Three: AN EXPLORATION OF GENDER	29
Girl OR Boy?	30

Beyond The Gender Binary   33

The Genderbread Person   34

My Gender Story   38

Gender and Pronouns   40

A Parent's Perspective: Meet Laurin Mayeno   42

Additional Resources   44

Chapter Four: UNDERSTANDING THE LGBTQ+ ALPHABET SOUP   47

Coming Out To Myself And My Parents   48

Identifying Our Biases   51

A Generational Shift   52

Sex, Gender Identity, And Sexual Orientation   53

Avoiding 6 Language Mistakes   58

Chapter Five: CREATING INCLUSIVE CLASSROOMS   61

The Tale Of Two Schools   62

1. Display Inclusive Signs In Your Classroom   63

2. Include Everyone In the Words You Use   64

3. Include Everyone In Your Curriculum   66

4. Take An Intersectional Approach to Inclusion   67

Change Starts In Your Classroom   69

Chapter Six: CREATING INCLUSIVE SCHOOLS   73

The Importance Of An Adult Ally   75

Changing A School's Culture   79

Change Is Possible If You Believe In It!   82

How To Start A GSA Club   **84**

The Kick-Off Meeting   *88*

Suggested GSA Topics & Activities   *88*

National Calendar   *89*

Be The Change You Want To See On Your Campus   **91**

Chapter Seven: PROFILE OF AN EXTRAORDINARY TEACHER   **92**

Interview With Bridey Thelen-Heidel   **93**

Carmela   *99*

Timothy/Samantha   *100*

Rafael   *100*

Tommy's Mom   *101*

Chapter Eight: CONCLUSION   **111**

About Sameer Jha & The Empathy Alliance   **113**

Acknowledgements   **115**

Author's Note

I still remember hiding under my best friend's bed, feeling guilty for playing with his younger sister's beautiful dolls. A few weeks earlier, on my fifth birthday, my parents had decided to box away my doll collection. They bought me a blue train set as a replacement, but no matter how much I tried to like it, I couldn't. So, I resorted to playing with dolls in secrecy, knowing what I was doing was wrong because other boys were not like me. Throughout my childhood, I was bullied for being who I was, and grappled with fear and shame because of it. When I finally came out in high school, I was fortunate to gain the support of my parents and find friends who accepted me unconditionally. My life changed for the better, but I knew other queer youth were not as lucky. I decide to make it my goal to create safer schools and communities for youth like me. My hope is to create a more inclusive world for all youth experiencing emotionally and physically traumatic bullying, rejection, and isolation. To that end, I founded a nonprofit called The Empathy Alliance when I was fourteen, to accelerate the acceptance of LGBTQ+ youth in schools across the country.

I am very proud that through The Empathy Alliance, I have reached over a million people with my message of empathy. Many of them are educators, student leaders and parents working to change their schools from within. I collaborate closely with other organizations focused on improving the inclusion of queer youth, like the Human Rights Campaign, GLSEN, the Tyler Clementi Foundation, GSA Network, and Trikone. These amazing organizations, as well as numerous mentors, have helped me develop my expertise in LGBTQ+ activism and education. Now, I facilitate workshops, speak on panels, give speeches, and write articles on anti-LGBTQ+ bullying in schools.

Creating change in my community, and seeing its impact on students' lives, has taught me the power of a single person's willingness to act. It inspires me to continue my work on a national scale. I have loved meeting educators who truly care about student well-being and go out of their way to gain the tools and knowledge they need to support LGBTQ+ youth. In my experience, supportive teachers, counselors, and school staff are the key to creating safe and inclusive schools. This book is inspired by such educators. Here, I have revealed many deeply personal stories about my childhood and coming out process to help provide context for the tips and tools I share. I hope you find the book valuable— thank you for taking the time to read it!

CHAPTER ONE

WHY THIS BOOK MATTERS

Huddled inside the bathroom stall, I listened to the receding footsteps until I knew I was alone. I unlocked the door and slowly emerged from the safety of my stall, taking a second to glance at my reflection in the mirror above the sink. I did my best to wipe the traces of dirt and tears from my face, as I didn't want to raise my mom's suspicions when she came to pick me up. If she asked questions, I knew my answers would upset her, and even though I was still shaking from the traumatizing encounter, I had to protect her from the truth.

I was in seventh grade at the time, doing a community service project with my Boy Scout troop. Our project brought us to my former elementary school where we were charged with planting a new garden. I was excited to give back to my community, while enjoying a nice day out in the sun with classmates.

Vibrant colors have always drawn my attention. The moment I saw the rows of flower pots with bright purple, red, and yellow plants, I knew exactly what I wanted to do. Daydreaming about how gorgeous the new landscape would look when we were done, I set to work making it happen. With both hands in the dirt, the project consumed all my focus, which is why I barely noticed that a group of boys from my troop had circled above me.

"What is this?" one of the boys sneered while kicking a small plant next to me.

Too excited to notice their mean tone, I said, "I think we should put this purple plant here. Purple is my favorite color."

"Purple! That's such a girly color! You're so gay!" one of the boys jeered.

"So gay!" the other boys chimed in. Since they all had shovels in their hands, I thought they must have come to offer help, but I had clearly misjudged why this gang of Boy Scouts had approached me.

"You're disgusting! You know that?" said one boy as he grabbed a handful of dirt from the pot of my purple plant and threw it at my face. The others laughed as I flinched, and they started jabbing the soil around me intimidatingly with their shovels.

Terrified and ashamed, I bolted as fast as I could away from the group of boys and from my landscaping masterpiece. I ran to the restroom, hoping they would not follow me.

By the time I got inside my mom's car, I had removed all traces of sadness and hurt and pretended like nothing had happened. I began to dread attending Boy Scout meetings and eventually quit the troop.

The Extent Of Bullying In Schools

In this chapter, we'll explore the obstacles LGBTQ+ students like me face, how LGBTQ+ bullying is different than other types of harassment, and why understanding this difference is key to protecting and supporting your LGBTQ+ students.

School can be a tough place for kids. Students try to fit in, or at least not stand out, just to avoid being bullied. The consequences of non-conformity can be especially severe for students who don't fall in line with traditional gender roles: "girl behavior" and "boy behavior." For LGBTQ+ youth, campuses across the country are often scary and hostile places. Students like me are subject to verbal taunts and even physical assault that can have lasting psychological consequences.

If you read the word "LGBTQ+" and asked yourself, "What does that alphabet soup of letters and a plus sign mean?" you're certainly not alone. I'll give more in-depth information about who makes up the LGBTQ+ community in Chapters 3 and 4. For now, all you need to know is that I'll use the acronym LGBTQ+ consistently throughout this book to refer to people with genders and sexualities that are discriminated against or considered different from the majority. The letters stand for Lesbian, Gay, Bisexual, Transgender, And Queer. The Q can also be used for Questioning, which means that a person is still trying to figure out their sexual orientation or gender identity. LGBTQ+ is the umbrella term I prefer to use for my community, although you may come across other acceptable variations such as GLBT, LGBT, LGBTQIA, as well as the umbrella word queer.

Through my activism within the LGBTQ+ community, I've had the privilege of speaking with youth across the nation representing every background you can imagine. I feel fortunate that they have opened up to me and have trusted me with their stories, many of which are harrowing accounts far worse than anything I have ever experienced. Many of my LGBTQ+ peers have dropped out of school as a result of the struggles they've faced, succumbing to depression and even contemplating the worst way out of their misery: suicide.

Sobering Statistics

Suicide is the second leading cause of death among all young people between 10 and 24 years old (accidents take the number one position). However, according to the Centers of Disease Control & Prevention, LGBTQ+ youth are nearly three times as likely to have seriously contemplated suicide and five times as likely to have attempted suicide as their non-LGBTQ+ counterparts. In addition, suicide attempts by LGBTQ+ youth are often much more harmful, requiring medical attention five times more often than attempts by non-LGBTQ+ youth.

GLSEN, an organization focused on LGBTQ+ issues in K-12 education, conducts a biennial National School Climate Survey of more than 10,500 students from all fifty states. Their findings are truly disturbing: 98% of LGBTQ+ students have heard "gay" used in a negative way. This was very common in my school, and I am sure you've probably heard a student (or even one of your colleagues) say "That's so gay!" as a way to express that something is stupid or silly. Students also reported hearing other types of homophobic and transphobic slurs such as "dyke, faggot, tranny, or he/she" and feeling distressed because of this language.

Verbal bullying can often escalate to something much more serious. More than a quarter of LGBTQ+ students were physically harassed in the past year because of their sexual orientation. 58% of LGBTQ+ students felt unsafe at school because of their sexual orientation, and 43% because of their gender expression. More than half of the LGBTQ+ students who were harassed or assaulted in school did not report the incident to school staff.

Let's think for a second about what it feels like to be an LGBTQ+ student in school. LGBTQ+ students are much more likely to disengage from school, lose interest, or even drop out because of all they have to deal with. Nearly one-third of LGBTQ+ students report missing school because they felt unsafe or uncomfortable. Even students who seem okay on the surface can carry heavy emotions like anxiety, fear, or shame.

One of my close friends from middle school recently came out to me as lesbian. She has not yet shared her sexual orientation with her classmates, and worries about what her parents will think if they find out the truth. When we talked about the lack of LGBTQ+ awareness we and our peers had in middle school, she made a very powerful statement about the one thing she would like to change about the past: "I wish that my middle school me knew it was ok to be who you are, and that being LGBTQ+ was not something you should be ashamed of."

All she wanted was the ability to be herself! It really is that simple. Sometimes as a teacher it may seem overwhelming to cater to the needs of different groups of students. However, just remember that LGBTQ+ students need the same thing all students need: a place where they feel safe enough to be themselves.

You Are Teaching LGBTQ+ Students

GLAAD, an organization that works to accelerate the acceptance of LGBTQ+ people in society, conducted a survey in 2017 to understand what percentage of the population identifies as LGBTQ+. They noticed that the younger you are, the more likely you are to openly identify as LGBTQ+ compared to older generations. Around 20% of millennials (18-34 years old) identify as LGBTQ+! This means it is very likely that you have someone in your classroom who is LGBTQ+, even if they don't realize it yet.

Did you know that LGBTQ+ related bullying doesn't just harm LGBTQ+ students? Heterosexual (straight) students who are perceived to be LGBTQ+ can become targets of bullying as well. A foundation of safety and security is essential for ALL students to fully realize their academic potential. Therefore, a good classroom must be inclusive of each and every student. Promote a classroom culture that is accepting of LGBTQ+ youth, with a learning mindset based on mutual respect regardless of differences among students.

To gain first-hand insight into the differences in the experiences of LGBTQ+ students and heterosexual, cisgender students, I conducted a survey in 2016, during my sophomore year. Cisgender is a term for people whose gender identity is male or female, and matches the sex they were assigned at birth. In the survey, I asked my fellow high school students to reflect on their middle school years. I posed questions such as "Did you or anyone in your school ever experience name-calling, bullying, or harassment as a result of actual or perceived gender identity or sexual orientation?" and "On a scale of 1 to 5, how satisfied were you with your middle school's programs to create a safer and more inclusive environment for LGBTQ+ students." 42 students representing 24 different middle schools in Northern California responded.

In my survey, 52% of total respondents and 65% of LGBTQ+ students said they or someone they knew in school had experienced name-calling, bullying, or harassment. The most surprising thing for me was the extent to which non-LGBTQ+ students were also impacted: 44% of them had personally experienced or witnessed harassment. They wanted a safer, more accepting school environment, and expressed their desire for teachers to act and provide information to combat negative stereotypes. They said that sometimes even if they were not LGBTQ+ the perception of being different from the rigid gender behaviors expected of boys and girls would make them a target of bullying.

I still remember one straight student who said that when it came to LGBTQ+ awareness their middle school did "nothing really." They wrote, "We actually completely avoided the conversation, and I thought that the words 'gay' and 'homosexual' were bad words until I came to high school. Because there was so much stigma associated with those words, no one in my school felt safe enough to come out." They went to a middle school in the San Francisco Bay Area! In what is called the gay capital of the world, even today, students experience anti-LGBTQ+ bullying.

In short, this issue impacts ALL students, in all classrooms, all over America—including yours.

"Gay" Should Not Be A Slur

Think back to your K-12 years. I'm sure all of you recall kids being bullied. Maybe you were the target of someone's mean words.

Perhaps you witnessed your peers making fun of others. Or, maybe you regret that the verbal taunts even came from you. Whatever the case, you understand one thing: words matter.

When I was with my Boy Scout troop doing community service, I was taunted as being gay. Though at its core the word gay means "attracted to the same gender," it was used as a slur (in a derogatory way) in my middle school and in schools across the country. This explains why the slur in the Boy Scout incident was followed up with "you're disgusting." I'm certain that all of you reading this book would agree that insulting students for something they can't control, something as simple as who they are attracted to (whether true, assumed, or anywhere in between), is unacceptable. Saying "that's so gay" is not okay!

A boring movie. An ugly outfit. A joke that's not funny. A terrible idea. A song you can't stand. These all share one common aspect: in the eyes of many kids and adults across the country, they're "gay". Gay in this context has little or nothing to do with sexual orientation or attraction. It's about something being silly, stupid, or even repulsive. So, in my examples a movie that's gay is one you didn't like. A joke that's gay fell flat. An idea that's gay is one that you think absurd. A song that's gay is one you never want to hear again.

Yet even though the word here isn't being used to describe sexual orientation, it is still extremely harmful for LGBTQ+ students to hear. As we discussed before, statistically it is very likely you have an LGBTQ+ student in your class. Though this child may or may not have realized their identity yet, imagine the association that they develop around the word "gay."

When the "G" in LGBTQ+ is synonymous with silly, stupid, or even repulsive, and a person hears gay used over and over again in this way, what do you think it does to this person's perception of LGBTQ+ people? After all, the reason why many people use gay to mean all these negative things comes from the belief some people hold that LGBTQ+ people are disgusting. If you and everyone in your classroom understands that using "gay" as a slur significantly impacts the health and safety of LGBTQ+ students, you can work to change the meaning of the word into an identity that is accepted and supported in your classroom.

What I Have Learned About Bullying

I already shared some of my experiences with bullying in middle school, but let me tell you a little more about that time. I spent my elementary and middle school years in a public-school system that drew its 90% Asian-American population from my suburban neighborhood. Academics were rigorous and intense, and students were driven to work hard and do well. I loved learning, enjoyed going to school, and had a great relationship with all my teachers. They were overworked and under-resourced, yet still always found time to mentor me. Despite my positive experiences in the classroom, my life outside became increasingly challenging.

I had always been a feminine kid who loved dolls, Disney princess songs, and glitter. When I was young, my friends and I would act out plots from our favorite TV shows on the wobbly stage at school during lunch. But as I grew older, boys wanted nothing to do with theatre. My male peers wanted to look tough, while I wanted to stay my fabulously flamboyant self. I was intensely bullied for my girly hobbies, high voice, and effeminate mannerisms. Some of my closest friends became my worst tormentors. Homophobic slurs were hurled at me before I even got a chance to think about my sexuality.

I don't want to give the impression that I was always unhappy. In fact, I was very fortunate in many ways! I loved reading and spent countless lunch periods in our school's library, finding a happy escape between the covers of a good book. As president of the Drama Club, I was also able to create an inclusive and welcoming space for other students who didn't fit the norm.

Together, we spent many enjoyable hours recreating talking forests, secret gardens, and mermaid lagoons.

At home, my mom and dad made it a point to provide a loving environment for me. They always told me they accepted me no matter what and taught me to be kind to all people. I know I'm luckier than many LGBTQ+ youth in this country, and I never take that for granted.

A few months after the Boy Scout incident, my parents and I attended a musical called *All Shook Up* based on the Shakespeare play *Twelfth Night*. In both productions, a man falls in love with a woman who is dressed like a man. Afterwards, my parents brought up the topic of sexuality, and at one point they said, "Sameer, even if you were gay, we would still love you."

Immediately, all the negative images I had about what "gay" meant shot rapid fire in my mind. My male peers had made it clear my feminine behavior was unacceptable because, in their eyes, it was gay. And being gay was, according to them, deserving of verbal and physical harassment. When you hear something like "that's so gay" every day, over and over, you start to believe it. So, when my parents brought up my sexuality, I immediately became defensive. Though their reassurance came from a place of love (and was concerning a hypothetical situation they did not really believe would come true), the word gay then felt exactly the same as when it was used to insult and bully me in the Boy Scout incident. I was being forced to confront my sexuality, and even defend it, before I truly understood what any of it meant. I assumed my parents and classmates saw something in me—something gay—that I should have hidden or repressed.

"No, I'm not! Why would you even say something like that?" I choked out. I remember feeling embarrassed, my heart beating in my chest and my throat closing up.

Today I can look back with humor at this incident, but at the time it felt very painful. Last year, I shared this story during a group activity at the annual Student Diversity Leadership Conference

(SDLC), a multiracial, multicultural gathering of 1,600 high school students from across the U.S. For me it was a time of self-reflection and personal growth as an activist, as well as an opportunity to learn from other student leaders.

One SDLC participant, Katia from Miss Porter's School in Connecticut, beautifully described the additional burden carried by many LGBTQ+ students: "I wish my teachers knew that even if I am in a safe/accepting space, there is an additional layer of internal oppression that I struggle with every day that continues to affect my social and educational experiences at school."

The weight of what is called internalized homophobia, the difficulty of accepting ourselves as LGBTQ+ because of how our society and community has trained us to think about our identities, is something commonly shared by many LGBTQ+ youth like myself. Because I associated the word gay with words like disgusting, silly, and stupid, my internalized homophobia stopped me from accepting myself and instead made me reject my identity.

So when you hear that something is "so gay," start with the premise that at least one student you've taught or will teach may identify as LGBTQ+. This student may not have come to understand it yet, but the words they hear spoken by their classmates and teachers will impact how and when they do come out. And when they do, think of being the amazing teacher that they recall shed a positive light on their identity by putting an end to anti-LGBTQ+ language.

As I can attest, if I had one teacher in my elementary or middle school who had taken a stand against the word gay (or dyke, faggot, and tranny) being used in a harmful way, that person would have been my hero for life, someone I'd never forget! They would have helped me see that the LGBTQ+ community, a community I now call my own, is amazing, not disgusting. If what you've read so far has motivated you to create lasting change within your classroom and campus, but you're unsure how to proceed, I hope this book can help.

In the next chapter, you'll learn how to make small but significant shifts in the way students behave around you. I'll provide a simple and immediately adoptable strategy to support your LGBTQ+ students. It begins with putting an end to using the word gay as a synonym for silly, stupid, or repulsive.

If you take away nothing else, just remember two key things:
1. You have at least one LGBTQ+ student, and they are listening to the words you, your colleagues, and other students use.
2. Your non-LGBTQ+ students will interact with LGBTQ+ people now and in the future, and will need to respect and support them.

The way you can help ALL your students, no matter what their sexuality or gender, is by setting a positive example with the words you say, and the words you condone.

CHAPTER TWO

PUTTING AN END TO ANTI-LGBTQ+ SLURS

T his chapter, in four words, is about *small but significant changes*. In future chapters, I will cover more involved strategies like starting an LGBTQ+ club and more complex topics like the use of gender neutral pronouns. However to make an immediate difference, all you need to do is prevent the most pervasive form of bullying: the common usage of anti-LGBTQ+ slurs. LGBTQ+ students almost universally report hearing verbal abuse like "gay," "dyke," "tranny," "homo," "faggot," and "sissy." What you may not know is how frequently this occurs. According to a 1998 study, the National Mental Health Association found students hear anti-gay slurs on average about 26 times a day. I would contend that even hearing such slurs once a day is enough to do irreparable damage to the mental and emotional wellbeing of students.

Have you ever heard these slurs being used by students or faculty members on your campus? If yes, take a few minutes to carefully write down a list of the words you've heard at your school that refer to someone's sexuality or gender in an insulting way. Now put a big, giant X through that list! I am convinced by research, my own personal experiences, and the heart-wrenching stories of others that the single most impactful thing a teacher can do to support

LGBTQ+ students is to put an immediate stop to the derogatory usage of words like "gay."

As a leader and role model for our students, you're influencing their behavior. So, you want to model LGBTQ+ acceptance by using appropriate language and speaking up when you hear slurs used. With that said, traveling across the country and speaking to thousands of educators has taught me that no two-school cultures are the same. Each teacher is amazing at some part of LGBTQ+ inclusivity (you included!), whether it is having a deep sense of responsibility and care for struggling students or teaching colleagues about different identities. And each teacher also has some area where they want to improve.

If you have already developed skillful and respectful ways to stop students from using all the slurs that you just listed, then bravo! You, and your school, seem to have policies in place to specifically address anti-LGBTQ+ bullying, and you can move on to learning about gender in the next chapter. But if you're looking for simple and effective strategies to support LGBTQ+ students and keep them safe, read on.

You Are Not Alone In This Journey

Before we jump to my recommendations, I would like to congratulate you on the journey you are about to start. You are making a decision to learn more about supporting LGBTQ+ youth, and that can seem like a daunting task to take on in addition to your current duties and responsibilities as a teacher. Luckily, you don't need to do this alone! There are numerous resources for educators available from credible, national LGBTQ+ organizations that have been tried and tested in schools with success. One such organization is The Human Rights Campaign (HRC), the largest LGBTQ+ civil rights organization in the United States.

I first learned about HRC through two amazing mentors, Beth Burkhart and Keely Stevenson, who connected me to Dr.

Vinnie Pompei. It was a chilly March day in San Francisco when Vinnie and I first met in a hotel lobby near Union Square. He needed to leave for the airport to catch a flight, yet his personality exuded a warmth and friendliness that felt the opposite of rushed. He encouraged me to get hot chocolate and a bagel, and waited patiently as if he had all the time in the world. I guess it must have been his decades of experience working with youth as a middle school teacher, a high school counselor, and now the Director of HRC's Youth Well-Being Project, because he immediately put me at ease.

We ended up spending a lot of time talking about the difference between equality and equity, two educational approaches for how to treat students fairly. Equality is about treating all students the same, but it only works if everyone starts from the same place. Equity assumes students have different circumstances and challenges, and emphasizes giving students what they need to be successful. For your LGBTQ+ students, the needs that differ from those of the rest of your students include protection from anti-LGBTQ+ bullying.

Vinnie chairs HRC's annual Time to Thrive conference. Time to Thrive is one of the largest national gatherings for educators interested in promoting equity for LGBTQ+ youth. Vinnie encouraged me to attend Time to Thrive in 2017, where I met hundreds of educators and mental health professionals, and HRC Youth Ambassadors, a group that I now belong to. If your budget allows, I would recommend that you attend this conference, as it offers inspiring keynotes, dozens of workshops, networking opportunities with fellow educators, and access to numerous organizations that offer resources for LGBTQ+ youth and their teachers. Occasionally, HRC offers scholarships and discounts to make Time to Thrive more accessible.

HRC also released a 2018 LGBTQ Youth Report in partnership with the University of Connecticut, that surveyed 12,000 LGBTQ+ teens between the ages of 13-17. I was one of the teens surveyed, along with youth from all 50 states: the extremely insightful results are available for free at www.hrc.org. These are just two resources for any educator interested in learning more about the realities of being an LGBTQ+ student in school. Be sure to also check out HRC's Welcoming Schools program website, which is full of professional development tools for educators looking to create a better, more accepting environment for their students. Their easily implementable strategies have worked in schools across the country.

In this book I have used suggestions from Welcoming Schools, as well as other groups that I have met because of my activism work. I especially want to acknowledge GLSEN, The GSA Network, The Tyler Clementi Foundation, and GLAAD as these organizations have given me valuable resources and training, supported my mission to end bullying in schools, and helped me amplify my voice and message. They will help you, just like they helped me. The websites of these organizations are brimming with teacher's guides and toolkits, and are worth checking out. You truly do not have to feel like you are alone in this journey.

Your school may already have LGBTQ+ initiatives in place, or it may be prepared to embrace an LGBTQ+ affirming program with the help of a concerned teacher like you. Sadly, some schools may be completely opposed to any program that deals with LGBTQ+ acceptance. In this chapter, I present basic tips that don't require a lot of time, resources, or school support—just your willingness as one teacher to make a difference in the immediate space around you. Once you understand how to approach anti-LGBTQ+ slurs and language, you can implement these strategies right away.

Interrupt + Educate Every Time You Hear Anti-LGBTQ+ Insults

The way we use language changes and evolves over time. The word gay used to just mean happy, and then it was used to describe people who experience same-gender attraction. Now it is often used as an insulting word that means silly, stupid, or repulsive, based on negative attitudes toward the LGBTQ+ community. We can all work together to change this word once again and prevent it from being used in ignorant and hurtful ways. Someone should be proud to be called gay, not think of this identity as an insult. A more positive association can only be created if we call out and reject the derogatory one.

STEP 1: Interrupt

Every time you hear words like "gay" used as a slur, call it out. Don't ignore it or gloss over it, because you don't want to give the signal that such language is acceptable. Here is some great advice from a straight student named Priya, who studies in a large public high school:

> *Often, I see students using words that are offensive,*
> *such as calling other students gay or tranny as an*
> *insult. I do know that teachers are aware of it, and I*
> *wish that teachers would stop being bystanders to*
> *this. If they overhear this/see it happening they*
> *should try to put a stop to it.*

As a teacher, one way to respond is with questions like:

- What do you mean by that?
- What were you trying to say when you used the word "gay" in that way?

Such questions can encourage students to think about why they used a slur and how they could use a different, more appropriate word next time. You can also make firm statements such as:

- We don't tolerate name-calling in our school.
- Using words like "dyke" or "tranny" is unacceptable and hurtful. Please apologize to your classmates.

These types of statements make it crystal clear that anti-LGBTQ+ slurs are not condoned. They demonstrate to students that you, as a teacher in a position of authority, do not accept language like this. In the specific context of your school, what are some ideas that come to your mind for how to stop students from thoughtlessly using anti-LGBTQ+ language? Please note your responses down so you can return to these ideas once you have finished reading the book.

Much of the name-calling behavior is automatic, like a bad habit. And habits are hard to change. Students have grown used to expressing themselves in a certain way simply because they, and those around them, have been doing so for a long time. Most of your students will probably not stop using the term gay in a harmful way by you pointing it out to them once. But while your campus culture won't transform overnight, with enough repetition and practice students will learn to change their language. This is why you need to continue to interrupt and call attention to the harmful slurs they use each and every time. Through repeated reminders, your words will eventually stick. You will have made your rules, and your expectations clear. Over time, your students will understand that you are a teacher who doesn't put up with harmful and hurtful language, and that you stand for the acceptance of all students.

STEP 2: Educate

While the negative use of "gay" can sometimes be an intentional attack against LGBTQ+ people, I believe that in the majority of cases, it comes from a lack of education and awareness. Students cannot change their behavior unless they truly understand its impact. During my work with straight and cisgender students, I have been struck by the fact that while they recognize that anti-LGBTQ+ slurs are negative, they see them as something more humorous than harmful.

One of my straight classmates from middle school recalls the school climate as "overall neutral" towards LGBTQ+ students. She admits, "People sometimes made offensive jokes, like calling people gay or faggot as an insult, but to my knowledge, this was the extent of such harassment. Many people, as I know them today, were and are accepting of LGBTQ+ students."

Can you really be an LGBTQ+ supporter and still use anti-gay insults? I will let others debate that, but I personally believe in giving my peers the benefit of doubt. Sometimes, it can be very hard for people to understand the deep emotional pain and shame that can come from hearing LGBTQ+ slurs when they have not felt it themselves. So, once you have interrupted a verbal harassment incident and have made it clear that it is unacceptable, try taking the additional step to explain why. Of course, this may not always be possible. For example, if you're in the middle of a math lesson and need to teach a complex concept by the time the bell rings, you probably don't have the time to delve into the implications of what it means when a student says that something is gay right there and then. But when you can, use an incident to spark a conversation or dialogue. Invite students to share their perspective, by asking them to reflect on things like:

- Why it is unacceptable to use words like gay, tranny, dyke, and fag negatively. What do they reflect about our values as a school community?
- What could be the potential impact on students belonging to gender or sexual minorities if they heard such language? Is that acceptable?
- Broaden the conversation to other types of slurs that students may have used or heard that make fun of someone's race, religion, abilities, or physical characteristics. Help draw parallels so students can learn to recognize patterns of bullying and discrimination.
- What do words like gay, lesbian, bisexual, and transgender really mean? Help students learn their proper and respectful usage. In Chapters 3 and 4, I will define all these terms in greater detail.

Your probing could encourage your students to provide their viewpoints. Some students who would otherwise remain silent may decide to share what's on their mind. Others may have never been pushed to think about the implications of their use of the word gay this way, and may ask questions that will help them learn.

I remember how surprised I first was when I learned that many incredible historical figures, people I could look up to and be proud of, may have been queer: Socrates, Aristotle, Plato. Alexander the Great, Leonardo da Vinci, Michelangelo, Alan Turing, Oscar Wilde, Lord Byron, Walt Whitman, Tennessee Williams, Hans Christian Andersen, Andy Warhol, Frida Kahlo, Eleanor Roosevelt, J. Edgar Hoover, Susan B. Anthony and more. I believe the queer youth of today also have the potential to become tomorrow's great philosophers, artists, poets, leaders, and scientists as long as they can be proud rather than ashamed or fearful of who they are. Note: I use the term queer throughout this book to mean someone who is not straight and cis, similar to the umbrella term LGBTQ+.

Another proactive approach to confronting this issue would be to register for GLSEN's No Name-Calling Week in mid January. The week is organized by K-12 educators and students leaders to end name-calling and bullying in schools. Registrants get access to free videos, classroom guides, and lots of grade-level appropriate resources that can help you shape your school's culture to be more inclusive.

Quick Update: In May 2018, almost six months after I wrote this chapter, I was invited to join GLSEN's National Student Council. During a strategy & planning session at their New York headquarters, I had to pick which committees I was interested in joining. For me it was easy to choose *No Name-Calling Week* as one of the major initiatives I wanted to support. If you decide to observe No Name-Calling Week at your school and have any questions or needs, please feel free to email me at empathyawareness@gmail.com and I will be thrilled to help out in any way I can!

When you take a stand against any students' negative behavior and choose to interrupt and educate, it may be the first time in your students' lives that anyone has brought attention to the hurtful words they are using. That in itself is significant. You are saying that under no circumstances is it acceptable to use words like "gay" in a harmful way. Just as racist and sexist words are hopefully never allowed in your classroom, anti-LGBTQ+ language isn't either. Your students may grow defensive or push back by saying, "I didn't mean anything by it." However, it is important to explain that regardless of their intention, such language is offensive to the LGBTQ+ community.

Every situation and student is different, which is why I'm not providing one-size fits all solutions. In the end, you know your students best. Some may be receptive to you teaching them about the harmful implications of their verbal harassment, while others will benefit simply from you quickly stopping their behavior without long explanations. If your actions make your stance on LGBTQ+ acceptance clear, that is all that matters. The end goal of how you respond to the harmful use of words like gay is to create a safe school environment where all students can thrive academically and socially. Bringing about awareness is the means to accomplish this objective.

Beyond "So Gay": When Bullying Escalates

On Wednesday, September 22, 2010 at 8:42 p.m., a freshman at the University of Rutgers posted on Facebook: "Jumping off the gw bridge sorry." Seven days later, on September 29, his body was found north of the George Washington Bridge where he took the 200-foot leap into the Hudson River below. The freshman's name was Tyler Clementi.

His story made national headlines after it was revealed that his roommate had used a webcam to secretly capture Tyler in an intimate moment with another man. His roommate had described what he had seen and posted it on Twitter just days before Tyler took his life.

We will never know exactly what was going through Tyler's mind as he stood on the edge of the G.W. Bridge. However, no one should have to feel unsafe in their own dorm room, or deal with such harassment and an invasion of privacy at the hands of their roommate. Whatever Tyler was experiencing that Wednesday evening, he felt the only way out of it was to take his life. His story is a reminder to all of us who advocate for LGBTQ+ youth that anti-bullying programs are critical and can literally save lives.

When you decide that you never want a student who takes a seat in your classroom to feel like Tyler Clementi did, you're taking on an enormous responsibility. You may be the only adult on your campus who LGBTQ+ students can trust, and your classroom may be the only one in which they feel safe. The role you play in your students' lives may mean they come to you seeking help when they're being bullied. Or, your heightened awareness of anti-LGBTQ+ bullying on campus may mean you'll identify bullying where your colleagues would be oblivious or even indifferent to it. This is a difficult undertaking, but that makes it even more important.

Sadly, many LGBTQ+ youth do not feel comfortable reporting bullying to teachers. For a long time, I told no one about having dirt and anti-LGBTQ+ language hurled at me while I was planting flowers in the school garden. At the time, I just wanted the incident to disappear as quickly as possible. The shame associated with being humiliated and called something I didn't want to be identified with motivated me to keep it under wraps. Telling an adult would have brought more attention to what had happened, and I didn't want my classmates to think I was weak or a tattletale. Our school had a lot of anti-bullying programs in place, but LGBTQ+

harassment was not specifically called out. In fact, I had never heard a teacher or staff member talk about LGBTQ+ people in any context, either in health classes or during history lessons. All my information (or rather misinformation) came from my similarly unaware peers. So, I didn't know much about LGBTQ+ people, and I didn't know which faculty member I could approach to talk about it. It was too embarrassing to even consider. Had I been in a school or social environment where anti-gay harassment was not tolerated, and LGBTQ+ identities were respected, I would probably have felt more empowered to take action or at least ask questions.

While nearly every school has some sort of guideline in place to address bullying, LGBTQ+ specific anti-bullying policies are far less common. Having a broad anti-bullying strategy may make it seem unnecessary to have a policy in place for a particular group of students. After all, one blanket policy covers every individual. But LGBTQ+ youth need their own specific set of anti-bullying guidelines for the following reasons:

- Bullied students may not be out to their classmates or parents. Without a process that is highly confidential, they may remain unwilling to come forward.
- Due to the stigma associated with queerness, some students may not want to describe what happened to them or report the bullying incident, even if they are actually straight.
- Students may believe that confiding in you about being bullied will come at great personal risk; they may be afraid of being judged by you and worry that their situation will worsen.
- Some students may be struggling with understanding their own sexual orientation or gender identity and feel too embarrassed and confused.

On TV and in books, I often see stereotypical portrayals of a student who is being bullied. However, the reality is there is no one 'type' of bullied student. It may not always be the kid who is struggling with academics, or who sits alone at lunch. Neither of those were true for me; to my parents, teachers, and friends, I was a motivated, happy, energetic theatre kid who loved ancient history and geeked out about physics. They did not see the immense pain and sadness I was hiding. So much of my energy was spent trying to fit in: I was always monitoring and self-policing how I walked and talked, what I wore, and what I shared with others. Still, something would always give me away and attract hurtful remarks like "Dude, that's so gay!" from people I thought were my friends.

The National Education Association (NEA), has provided guidelines and practical online tools for educators to address LGBTQ+ bullying that will help you identify and help bullied students. I have added my perspective on some of their recommendations below:

Never Ignore Complaints
Students may be reluctant to tell you they're the victims of anti-LGBTQ+ bullying. It takes enormous courage to step forward and share experiences, especially when the stakes feel so high. Ignoring bullying as "boys being boys" or typical adolescent behavior, sends the wrong signal. Victims of bullying may interpret your silence or lack of action as you condoning anti-LGBTQ+ harassment. When students believe their safety is in danger, bullying takes on far greater significance. Something that may not seem as a big deal could have grave consequence for the student.

Listen and Protect
It isn't easy for victims of bullying to seek your help, so be as open and accepting as you can. Treat whatever they tell you as a privileged conversation, and do not share without their permission. They may be afraid of peer backlash if anyone found out they reached out to you. Let the student know that as long as there is no imminent threat of danger and what is disclosed does not fall under your school district or state's mandatory reporting guidelines, you'll only tell the people whom they've given you permission to talk to.

If you witnessed bullying but the victim hasn't come to you for help, make sure you approach them in a private setting where other students can't overhear. That way the student will have an easier time telling you what happened. Each situation will be different, so be patient as you encourage the student to open up to you and take your time to understand their needs. Don't assume that the victim identifies with the LGBTQ+ community—many straight students are subjected to anti-gay name calling. Even if they do identify, they may not be out to their parents or classmates and may fear exposure.

Report the Bullying

If the student gives you permission, report the incident to the appropriate authority in your school. If the harassment and the impact it has on your student falls within your school district or state's mandatory reporting guidelines, you need to report regardless of whether you receive permission—safety has to be your priority. The NEA suggests involving your school district's Title IX grievance officer. Make sure you communicate with the victim so they understand the process and feel supported and validated throughout. It may help to keep records of the incident as well, so you can refer to your notes later on. In cases of serious bullying, documenting what you witnessed or what the student reported is important.

Seek Professional Help

If you believe the student is experiencing emotional distress, provide resources for professional support. If you are not a trained mental health professional, you may want the student to speak to someone who is, such as the school counselor. If you believe the student is in immediate physical danger, reach out to your administration right away.

Prevention: Stop Bullying Before It Starts

Tyler Clementi's death placed the national spotlight on the impact bullying has on the LGBTQ+ community. In 2011, his family established the Tyler Clementi Foundation to "end offline and online bullying."

In the spring of 2017, the Tyler Clementi Foundation invited me to participate in a focus group that included twelve other LGBTQ+ activists from different parts of the United States. I arrived at the meeting wearing my favorite shirt, pale blue with a giant rainbow heart in the middle, and settled into a large comfy armchair. We introduced ourselves, and a coordinator from the foundation described the latest campaign they were launching, called #Day1. The premise of #Day1 was brilliant: What if we could prevent bullying before it starts? With that question, I was immediately hooked.

Focusing on prevention is important for the following reasons:
- By the time a teacher realizes a student is being bullied or harassed, it may be too late. Adults are often unaware of the dynamics within student groups. And bullying victims are often reluctant to report bullying for fear of repercussions associated with being labeled a snitch or a tattletale. By the time a teacher catches a bullying incident, it may have been taking place for a long time and victims may have experienced irreparable harm to their emotional or physical well-being.
- Many times, bullying occurs unintentionally. Students are often unaware that their joking and teasing is harmful.
- All parties involved in bullying, including bullies and bystanders, can be negatively impacted.

One of my favorite aspects of the #Day1 program is a pledge participants sign where they promise to be an upstander rather than a bystander. According to the Tyler Clementi Foundation, an upstander:

- Will stand up to bullying in all situations
- Will work to make others feel safe and included by treating them with respect
- Will not use demeaning language, slurs, gestures, facial expressions or jokes about anyone's sexuality, gender, race, size, religion, class, politics, or any kind of disability or differences, in person or online

During our focus group meeting we discussed the best way to introduce this anti-bullying program to students, how to strengthen the campaign language, and improve some of the social media strategies for maximum impact. After the focus group, I knew two things. The first was that I wanted to bring #Day1 to my own high school's GSA. The second was that I wanted to continue my involvement with the Tyler Clementi Foundation to help create positive cultural change in schools.

A month later, I was invited to be an inaugural member of the Tyler Clementi Foundation Youth Ambassador team. It has been a great learning experience for me to work closely with the Foundation and provide my perspective and insights on what is basically a free bullying prevention toolkit for teachers and students around the country. It has made me very happy to see the #Day1 program and other anti-bullying initiatives launched by the Tyler Clementi Foundation grow successfully and get adopted in an increasing number of schools.

The Ripple Effect

Creating a campus environment where students feel safe is essential for their well-being and academic success. Students who are preoccupied with fears of being bullied for their real or perceived LGBTQ+ identity are less focused on their classroom performance and more worried about their safety. Think of all that lost academic potential. In the case of Tyler Clementi, by his freshman year of college, he was already an accomplished violinist, selected to play in the university orchestra whose chairs were mostly filled by graduate students. Had Tyler not reached a breaking point that compelled him to take his life, we can only imagine what contributions he would have made using his gifts.

Sadly, so many LGBTQ+ students are put in this position, with two paths forward. One path is a life where one is given the support to achieve one's potential. I can attest to the priceless gift of a supportive family and loving teachers: this has allowed me to harness and develop my talents despite facing anti-LGBTQ+ bullying. And if you've ever seen any of the videos produced by Dan Savage's "It Gets Better Project," I'm sure you've been amazed at all the contributions members of the LGBTQ+ community have made to society. These tough, resilient, compassionate people have overcome obstacles and have made it to adulthood, offering messages of hope and inspiration to LGBTQ+ youth across the world.

That is unless they are on the other path, full of despair and misery that clouds one's ability to view the world through hopeful lenses. Many LGBTQ+ individuals see no respite from the struggles they encounter. They may have been rejected by their families, schools, and communities. They may be surviving on the streets—in fact, LGBTQ+ youth are 120% more likely to become homeless, according to a study from the University of Chicago. They may turn to drugs and alcohol for relief. Many have contemplated suicide, and many have actually taken their own lives.

Students, by themselves, cannot end LGBTQ+ bullying. And teachers alone cannot either. Both must work together to put a stop to the anti-LGBTQ+ words and actions that cause young people to cut short their potential by committing suicide, or by more subtle means, through the constant and steady erosion of one's self-worth that wears away at optimism, happiness, and a desire to succeed.

When even one teacher takes a strong anti-bullying stance, the entire campus culture shifts. This collective change goes for both the victims and perpetrators of anti-LGBTQ+ behavior. Those on the receiving end of bullying know they have a means to address the abuse and improve their lives. Meanwhile, the bullies realize their actions have immediate consequences. I've witnessed this remarkable transformation at my old middle school, a story I'll share in greater detail as a case study in Chapter 6.

While your campus culture may not be prepared to embrace a school-wide LGBTQ+ awareness strategy, what you've learned in this chapter will allow you to take charge of your immediate sphere of influence. Within your classroom, you have the ability to take a stand every day and create a safe space where all your students know they are supported and have the freedom to learn without fear of being harassed. Now that you know you can make a difference and change your student's lives, let's explore gender and sexuality, and how understanding these identities can help you support ALL of your students.

CHAPTER THREE

AN EXPLORATION OF GENDER

Ninety nervous teens, myself included, walked down a dirt path leading to the clearing full of cabins where we would be staying for the next two days. My new classmates and I were excited to get to know each other, the peers we would be spending the next four years with at our new high school. Once we stepped off the bus, we were welcomed by a group of seniors charged to lead our orientation retreat. "You're going to have a great time!" they reassured us.

I felt reluctantly optimistic. Would my new school setting provide a more open environment, where I could fully be myself and not have to worry about being called 'gay' all the time? A part of me was already missing my drama club teammates and other close friends who would all be going to a high school 5 minutes from my house. Still, as I looked at the incredible diversity of my new freshman class, I felt very hopeful. After all, The College Preparatory School had a reputation for making diversity a priority, so maybe the daily two and a half hour commute was worth it.

The retreat was jam-packed with activities that allowed us to learn about one another and build trust. We shared meals, participated in games, and had a talent show. Hesitantly, I signed up to sing a song at the talent show that I had written over the summer. My classmates supportively cheered me on, and several people came up afterwards to introduce themselves. I soon started feeling very much at home.

On the second day of the retreat, as a final activity, we gathered together and reflected on our orientation experience. One courageous student volunteered to share something personal:

> I identify as non-binary, which means I don't feel like a boy or a girl. I would love if you could use they/them pronouns for me. I know it can be confusing and difficult, so I appreciate your support.

I sat respectfully silent, but inside, a series of thoughts swirled in my mind as I wondered about what the student had just said. What does all this mean? Non-binary? They/them pronouns? Rather than risk sounding ignorant by asking clueless questions, I waited to return home and then turned to the all-knowing internet for answers. On the first day of class, my English teacher also introduced herself by saying she used she/her pronouns. I learned that this helped normalize pronouns and allowed trans students to easily communicate their identities. This was the beginning of my journey of uncovering a completely new way of thinking about gender—information that has helped me better understand myself, too. In this chapter, I will share what I discovered, and how it's relevant to the work you do every day in the classroom.

Girl OR Boy?

Female or Male? Boy or Girl? Feminine or Masculine? You'll often hear people use these terms interchangeably, but in reality they represent completely distinct concepts. Understanding these differences is crucial to supporting your LGBTQ+ students.

Let's start with the most common question that expecting parents get asked is "Is it a boy or a girl?" We try to put a label on the child before it is even born. What we are really asking about is the biological sex of the child, and the answer carries significant weight.

Today, with feminism and gender fluidity constantly in the media, it may be easy to think we are living in a society where gender doesn't matter. Yet, a child's sex at birth still dictates the way they are raised and the roles they are trained to take on. We still encourage our boys to get dirty, play sports, act tough, and "be a man." These seemingly harmless words teach boys to hide and repress their emotions, and not to turn to others for support even during difficult times. Strength and power are still seen as the male ideals, and video games and action movies reinforce this view.

Girls are increasingly given strong female role models to replace the outdated damsel in distress figures that taught them to leave the action to men. However, girls are still labeled as aggressive for playing sports or bossy for taking leadership positions, and they still have Disney movies and coming of age teen flicks that focus on getting the guy. Even today, women continue to feel like they have to be the ones to take on the "rewarding" role of mother. If they want to pursue a challenging career they will be met with doubt and double standards (also lower salaries and success) the whole way.

Men also struggle in our society where they fear crying or showing vulnerability, knowing they will be seen as weak or less of a man. Instead they bottle up their emotions in unhealthy ways, sometimes acting out in anger and frustration against those closest to them. We are seeing more recognition of the downsides of this 'toxic masculinity' in books, TV shows and documentaries.

This division of the human race, at least in a Western context, into two distinct roles is what is referred to as the gender binary. It is based solely on the biological sex of a person at birth—what genitalia they possess. Our culture and society has taken these reproductive organs and built ridiculous mythologies around them that have little to do with reality. But how do we know that what we think of as feminine and masculine is an artificial social construct?

Let's take gendered clothing as an example. Today in the U.S., we would consider suits and polo shirts menswear, and dresses and skirts womenswear. But in India, my motherland, men wear elaborately embroidered pink and purple 'kurtas' that look more like knee length dresses. Not only is there variation in clothing for different genders around the world, but also right here in the United States. We just need to go back in time! According to the Smithsonian Magazine, a June 1918 article from the trade publication Earnshaw's Infants' Department said:

"The generally accepted rule is pink for the boys, and blue for the girls. The reason is that pink, being a more decided and stronger color, is more suitable for the boy, while blue, which is more delicate and dainty, is prettier for the girl." Filene's in Boston, Best & Co. in New York City, Halle's in Cleveland, and Marshall Field in Chicago all told boys to wear pink.

Let us look at the picture from 1884 of Franklin D. Roosevelt, 32nd President of United States (Source: Smithsonian Magazine). At age two, he can be seen with long hair, a feathered hat, and patent leather shoes. He is wearing a white frock that was standard, gender neutral clothing for both boys and girls at that time. He is dressed like most young children of his era. By today's standards though, many would assume they were looking at a girl instead of a boy.

Going back a few more centuries, in Europe we would have found aristocratic men who loved their high heels, lavish wigs, and makeup. In fact, from 4000 BC until the 18th century makeup was a common, often essential part of male grooming. Eye liner, eye shadow, face powder, lip color, blush, and paint for bald spots were all part of men's beauty routines.

Beyond The Gender Binary

In different cultures, and during different historical periods, the definition of what is appropriate for a boy or a girl varies. And this is just considering the societies that only recognize two genders. A look at Native American and Pacific Islander cultures can also help dispel the myth that all societies follow the Western system of dividing the human population into only two genders. There is evidence that more than one hundred and fifty Native American tribes culturally accepted the existence of a third and fourth gender, sometimes known as 'two-spirit.' Importantly, there was no requirement for a person of a third gender to have any visible biological basis for their identity: it could be something they discovered through visions or dreams. In my homelands of India and Pakistan, before the British colonization of South Asia, a third gender was also recognized in 'hijra' and 'khwaja sira' identities.

It would seem that even if biological sex at birth—what the doctor looks at to declare boy or girl—is fixed and binary, everything else is just a social construct. Yet, even sex at birth is not binary. Every year we have tens of thousands of babies born intersex. A study conducted by Brown University researcher Anne Fausto-Sterling showed that 1 in 100 births result in a baby whose body differs from the standard male or female. That's 1% of the population! That's the same as the percentage of redheads in the world.

So why do we persist in using the gender binary for all human beings? It seems that this social construct just impedes girls from achieving their true potential and prevents boys from experiencing and expressing their rich emotions. And what about everyone left out of this picture?

Instead of a rigid gender binary, many experts now believe that we should think of people as falling somewhere on a gender continuum or spectrum. Remember my freshmen classmate who shared that they identified as non-binary? When someone is non-binary, they don't feel like they fit the traditional definitions of being a girl or a boy, or they don't think of themselves as either gender. This can be very confusing; I know for me it definitely was! But with an open mind, let's now explore four important concepts that may help us view gender in new ways.

The Genderbread Person

One of my favorite ways to explain gender is using the learning tool of The Genderbread Person (Source: www.genderbread.org). It simplifies **sex** as what is between your legs, **identity** as what is in your mind, **expression** as what you wear on your body, and **attraction** as what is in your heart. Let us go a little deeper to fully understand and appreciate the nuances between these four terms.

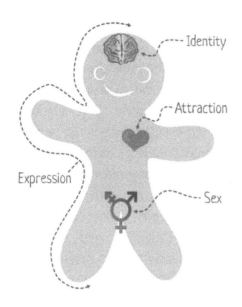

1) Biological or Assigned Sex: This is what goes on the birth certificate. Newborns are assigned a sex by the doctor based on anatomical appearance. AMAB stands for assigned male at birth, while AFAB stands for assigned female at birth. Actual biological sex is much more complex and includes chromosomes, hormones, and internal reproductive organs. Many babies are born intersex and do not biologically fit into the categories of male or female. Tragically, for decades doctors in America have been performing medically unnecessary surgeries on intersex babies to normalize their appearance and make them conform to one of the two sexes— often without parents being fully aware of the consequences. Biological sex just isn't naturally as binary as we like to think. Further, most of the things we associate with being male or female actually aren't about sex, but are about gender identity or expression.

Key terms: male, female, intersex

2) Gender Identity: If biological sex is about what is between the legs, then gender identity is about what is in our head. Some people's assigned sex and gender identity are pretty much the same, or in line with each other. These people are called cisgender. If you were assigned female and feel like a woman, you would be cisgender. Other people feel that their assigned sex is the opposite of their gender identity (i.e. assigned female at birth, but gender identity is a man). These people are called transgender or trans. Both these identities fall within a gender binary world with two assumed gender identities: man/boy and woman/girl. Note that we use man/woman when discussing gender identity, and the more biologically based male/female when talking about a person's sex.

However, gender can be more like a spectrum with many people finding themselves with identities that are neither fully feminine, nor fully masculine. Such people would still fall under the umbrella of transgender, because their gender identity doesn't match their sex at birth. They could use words like non-binary, gender expansive, genderfluid, or genderqueer to describe themselves.

I was fortunate to be able to speak on a panel of non-binary Youth Ambassadors at a Human Rights Campaign conference in Orlando recently. The panel took place during a lunch plenary session attended by almost one thousand educators and youth serving professionals, showing the increased interest in this topic. Hearing everyone's different experiences and conceptions of their gender identity just reinforced the fact that gender is complex and personal, but very important to trans people. That is why it is so critical to take the time to learn about how to support trans students in the classroom.

There are many words that people use to describe their own gender identity, and while the labels may feel overwhelming or seem confusing, the important thing to understand is that a person's biological sex may not line up with how they think about their gender. Scientific and psychological research has proven that trans people exist, and studies have shown that today's youth are more open to exploring and accepting gender fluidity and different identities. So it is important that you, as their teacher, learn a few ways to support them. If a person shares a gender identity that seems unfamiliar, don't be afraid to ask, "What does this term mean to you?" or "I'm not familiar with this identity, and if you feel comfortable sharing, I would love to learn more."

Lastly, let's clear a few things up. One: it's never too young for a child to identify as trans. As soon as they can communicate, many trans kids express their desire to be seen as their true gender. Two: you don't need to fear making mistakes. Trans people understand that it will be difficult to get used to a new way of seeing them. As long as you show your care and acceptance, you will do fine. Three: the words tranny, shemale, and hermaphrodite are not acceptable ways to refer to trans or intersex people. If you hear these words being used, even as a joke, take steps to ensure your students know how harmful these slurs can be. All the things we learned in chapters one and two about stopping name calling apply to insults against gender identities as well as sexual orientations.

Key terms: man, woman, cisgender, transgender, non-binary

3) Gender Expression: This is how we express our identity to society, including the clothes we wear, the way we talk, hairstyles, and mannerisms. As anyone who has scanned Amazon's toy section can attest, our understanding of gender expression is introduced to us from birth. Dolls and dresses are feminine, while swords and cars are masculine. There are endless examples of how we're conditioned to express our gender. And, as we've seen, gender expression changes based on context and history. Gender expression is how we interpret people's gender identity from the outside, but it doesn't tell us much more than how a person chooses to dress or act. So, it's best not to assume gender based on appearance alone. Many trans and nonbinary people have feminine and masculine elements in their expression, and this combination is called androgynous.

Others have an expression that is gender neutral, like short hair, a t-shirt, and jeans, which could be either feminine or masculine.

In Western society today, it is much more acceptable for girls to wear pants and like the color blue than it is for boys to wear dresses and like the color pink. As such, LGBTQ+ bullying can be particularly vicious when directed at feminine boys. All the bullying I experienced was because of my gender expression: I liked theatre, played with dolls, and spoke in a high voice. Try to help your students understand that boys should be allowed to be feminine. Traits that we consider feminine are just societal constructs forcing narrow role definition on us that are more harmful than helpful. Also, you may want to explore with your students why feminine behavior in boys is seen as a sign of weakness rather than strength. Could this be a form of misogyny where we consider anything associated with girls/women to represent less strength, courage, intelligence, willpower, and worth compared to boys/men?

Key terms: feminine, masculine, androgynous, gender neutral

4) Attraction: Attraction, or sexual orientation, is about what is in our hearts. It has nothing to do with one's own gender identity or gender expression. Rather, it's about who we love (romantic attraction) or who we may want to have sex with (sexual attraction). It is impossible to look at someone's outward mannerisms or clothing and know definitively who they are attracted to! We'll discuss attraction and sexual orientation in depth in the next chapter.

My Gender Story

While people who grow up fitting into society's binary gender roles may not think much about problems related to gender, those who struggle with conforming to these rigid binary standards are often subject to shame and ridicule. In my case, from a young age, I always knew I was different from my male peers. I would spend hours playing with Barbies and prancing around in my Cinderella dress and faux glass slippers. I quickly figured out my taste in toys and clothes would subject me to ridicule from other boys, so I'd hide my guilty pleasures from them. For this reason, I liked spending time with girls who enjoyed dressing up and playing with dolls. I loved using my imagination to create worlds I'd act out with my friends, and I enjoyed singing Disney songs, which was definitely frowned upon by most of my male peers. When it came to video games, I didn't get why anyone would pick a game where you'd shoot people or run them over with your tanks when you could choose one that allowed you to play the role of a fashion designer starting out her dazzling career in New York City. The majority of the media I consumed during my elementary school years was targeted at teenage girls and therefore featured teenage girls as main characters. I was especially a big fan of Hannah Montana. Who wouldn't want to lead a double life as a high school student and a world-famous pop star? I remember fantasizing about one day having the same experiences that the female characters I admired on TV did. At least until I realized that as a boy, I was supposed to identify with being the main character's male love interest rather than the star herself. My parents appreciated my sensitivity, and approved that I stayed away from violent video games, nerf gun wars, and the kind of rough play common among other boys in our neighborhood. Yet, they were afraid that I would be bullied for being different and their fears came true. The troubles I encountered with my gender expression plagued me throughout my elementary and middle school years. Whether it was group projects, PE, or even neighborhood gatherings, I didn't fit in with other boys. I was left out and, despite my parent's support, I felt increasingly alienated and ashamed for who I was and what I enjoyed doing. On one hand, I definitely wanted to fit in with my male peers. On the other, it felt unfair to be rejected for not conforming to narrow standards of boy behavior and girl behavior. As you know from the first chapter, the bullying I faced was physical and emotional, and really impacted my childhood. Yet once I came to the inclusive College Preparatory School, I was able to explore my own gender identity. I identify as agenderflux, which to me means I don't think of myself as a man or a woman or any combination of these, but just Sameer. The 'flux' part means how masculine or feminine I feel or want to present can change day to day. One day I can wear a dress and makeup, and another day I would feel more comfortable in a t-shirt and sweatpants. Also, I use both he/him and they/them pronouns. Now, this last section on pronouns is what many cisgender people find the most confusing about gender. But, if you read it and really take it to heart, you will have a great foundation to show respect and love for your trans students.

Gender and Pronouns

Imagine the name on your birth certificate said Thomas. But you always went by Tom. In fact, you really didn't like how Thomas sounded and hearing people call you Thomas bothered you. When you looked in the mirror you were Tom, not Thomas. Tom just felt right. Now let's say you met someone. You introduced yourself as you always did.

"Hi, I'm Tom," you said.

"Great to meet you. If you don't mind, I'm going to call you Thomas," she replied. You're confused. No one has ever said that to you.

"May I ask why you'll call me Thomas?"

"Well," she said, "Because growing up, I was told to always use the name Thomas. It's the correct and proper form. So I've stuck to that rule and that's why I refuse to call you Tom. And besides, is it such a big deal?"

I think we'd all agree that this person's argument is pretty disrespectful. And if she continued to use Thomas despite Tom's insistence to do otherwise, we'd probably say she was being rude.

Correct names and pronouns are extremely important when referring to a trans person. If a trans boy (this means he was assigned female at birth but identifies as a boy) who used to be called Ashley and used female (she/her) pronouns now wants to be called Louis and use male (he/him) pronouns, you should respect that. Try as hard as you can to use what he tells you to. Again, mistakes happen and that's okay.

In case you're confused about the way I'm referring to pronouns, "he/him" or "he/him/his" just means that the person wants you to say "He's a really passionate student, and his classmates love him." when talking about him rather than "She's a really great student..."

However, female pronouns (she/her) and male pronouns (he/him) can be problematic for those who identify as non-binary. If your sex says you're male, but your gender identity says you're non-binary, then being referred to as he or him may not match your own perception of who you are. At the same time, she or her may not fit as well. My non-binary classmate preferred that we use they/them instead of he/him or she/her pronouns. But how does that work? Isn't "they" plural? Some people may object and say, "That's so unnatural! I can't imagine referring to one person as 'they' or 'them.'"

Here's an example where we commonly do exactly that: You're driving a car. Suddenly, you see another driver weaving in and out of lanes recklessly. But you can't identify the driver's gender. In which case, you'll most likely say, "What the heck are they doing?" (Feel free to replace "heck" with a word that would get your students in detention if they blurted it out in class.) This comes naturally. You'd never say, "What the heck is he or she doing?" And for those that say this is grammatically incorrect or that they can't be expected to change the way English works, here's an example from the historical record:

"There's not a man I meet but doth salute me

As if I were their well-acquainted friend."

A quote by none less than William Shakespeare in *The Comedy of Errors*. So if Shakespeare (and Austen and Chaucer) can use singular they/them pronouns, you can too. However, if you feel like you need additional information, check out the awesome website iheartsingularthey.com.

A Parent's Perspective: Meet Laurin Mayeno

I first got to know Laurin Mayeno in her role as an author of a bilingual children's book *One of a Kind, Like Me/Único como yo*. I am always on the lookout for LGBTQ+ friendly literature, so I purchased the book, which she kindly signed for me. It was about a child named Danny who tells his mom he wants to be a princess in a school parade, and their quest for the perfect purple dress. When I read the actual story, I felt like the main character could have been me! It was a true story based on Laurin's experiences with her own gender non-conforming son. Laurin and I connected over email, and we have kept in touch ever since: she supports my activism efforts, speaks at events I organize, introduces my parents to other Asian LGBTQ+ families, and provides great advice whenever I need guidance.

I am fortunate to call her my mentor, because Laurin is also a sought after expert in the area of fostering LGBTQ+ inclusion and equity. She runs the Mayeno Consulting Firm, has co-founded Somos Familia (serving the Latina/o/x LGBTQ+ communities), and is an active leader within parent groups like the Asian Pacific Islander Rainbow Parents. So, I am really excited that Laurin agreed to provide us with a parent's perspective for this book.

Laurin shares, "Being Danny's mom, I have learned to appreciate children who don't follow expectations based on gender.

I also have seen how pressure to fit gender expectations can make life hard for any child. We can help all children feel safe and accepted by allowing them to explore a full range of activities without restricting or criticizing what they do based on gender. We can also make a difference by encouraging children to be respectful and kind to their peers, and by letting them know that teasing and bullying hurt. If you have a child who doesn't follow society's gender norms, rest assured that you are not alone. It is perfectly healthy to explore different ways of expressing gender." Below is a short recap of my interview with Laurin.

Sameer Jha: As a parent of a gender expansive child, what are the unique needs of LGBTQ+ students that teachers should be aware of?

Laurin Mayeno: LGBTQ+ students need safe havens. They need places where they can be who they are and know they are safe from bullying, judgment and stigma. When these safe spaces are lacking, they need support in navigating unsafe terrain and making choices that will help protect them from harm. Especially if they are in conservative areas, they may lack access information. They may not understand the feelings they are having and may think that something is wrong with them. They need support in developing resilience and pride in who they are. They need caring adults who affirm them for who they are. They need to know that they aren't alone. They need peers who support them. They need information and people to talk to so they can freely explore, affirm, and express their identities.

SJ: Are there simple things teachers can do immediately for their students that do not require a lot of resources?

LM: Assume that there are always LGBTQ+ students in your classroom, even if they aren't open about their identities. Use inclusive language and try to avoid making assumptions based on gender. For example: don't say "boys and girls", because this excludes people who are non-binary. Don't assume you know someone's gender based on how they look.

- Establish classroom norms around mutual respect, and no name-calling.
- Encourage learning and conversation about differences.
- Participate in activities such as No Name-Calling Week and Pride Month.
- Interrupt disrespectful behavior, such as name calling and mis-gendering.
- Be tuned in to students who may be experiencing depression, trauma, or bullying and find ways to offer them support.

SJ: Why is an inclusive and accepting school environment better for ALL students and not just those who belong to gender or sexual minorities?

LM: All students are impacted by gender and anti-gay stereotypes and bullying. These create a climate of fear and inhibit students feeling of safety, self-expression, and learning.

To learn more about Laurin's perspective, visit the websites for *Mayeno Consulting* and *Out Proud Families* and check out her blog. Also, google The New York Times short animation on Laurin Mayeno and her son called *A Mother's Promise.* It is the beautiful, emotional, and pretty unforgettable story of how she found the strength and love to accept her son.

Additional Resources

There are many amazing resources for you to get more than just this basic overview of gender. I have listed a few of my favorites below:

1. Gender Spectrum is a group whose "mission is to create a gender-inclusive world for all children and youth" has a large body of resources to help teachers, some of which I used in this section. You can learn about their trainings and programs at www.genderspectrum.org.
2. George by Alex Gino is a book aimed at middle school readers. It really explains the trans youth perspective beautifully.
3. My friend and fellow HRC Youth Ambassador Jazz Jennings has written a storybook *I Am Jazz* based on her own experiences as a trans child. Common Sense Media rates it as age appropriate for ages four and above. Recently, I joined a few other LGBTQ+ activists to raise enough funds to donate *I Am Jazz* books to every elementary school library in our city.
4. To learn more about how gender roles today harm even cisgender students, watch *Miss Representation* and *The Mask You Live In*, both of which are by The Representation Project and are available to stream on Netflix.
5. Another documentary available on Netflix is *Gender Revolution, A Journey With Katie Couric*. It shows a straight, cisgender Katie Couric's efforts to evolve her understanding of gender through a series of interviews with transgender and intersex individuals and their families.
6. *The Gender Creative Child: Pathways for Nurturing and Supporting Children Who Live Outside Gender Boxes* is an easy to read book by developmental and clinical psychologist Diane Ehrensaft. It covers the latest cultural, medical, and legal knowledge regarding transgender youth and is brimming with remarkable real stories. This is the first book I gave to my mom to help her accept and understand me better.
7. Finally, Laurin Mayeno's book *One of a Kind, Like Me/Único como yo* can help spark conversations about

gender diversity and appreciation of differences in elementary school settings. I love that it is bilingual, and also that it celebrates and normalizes femininity in boys.

In Chapter 4 we will explore sexual orientations and understand how they are different from gender identities. We will also learn tips for making classrooms more inclusive for all LGBTQ+ students, and finally get a handle on how each of the letters in that acronym are defined.

CHAPTER FOUR

UNDERSTANDING THE LGBTQ+ ALPHABET SOUP

From my first day of high school, I knew I was attending the perfect place for me. I loved my passionate teachers, my intellectually stimulating classes, and my diverse classmates. I immediately auditioned for the school play, *A Tale of Two Cities,* and was thrilled to get a role. Theater had always been my passion and I'd always bonded with theatre kids. Soon, a few of us became a tight-knit group. We regularly ate lunch together, helped each other with homework, and chatted outside of school. During lunchtime one day, I approached our usual lunch spot and saw four of my theatre friends huddled around a small smartphone screen.

"OMG saaame!" one said. They all burst out laughing as they watched a clip together.

"What are you looking at?" I asked. They explained they were watching a series of coming out jokes.

"It's National Coming Out Day," one of my friends pointed out to me. I already knew she was bisexual, as she had confided this to me during our second week of classes. However, I was stunned to learn that three of my theatre friends identified with sexualities other than straight. I was basically an LGBTQ+ magnet. I was naive and did not recognize what now seems so obvious—I was drawn to people like me. Through my friends, I started forming an understanding of the different LGBTQ+ identities. In this chapter, you'll learn what they mean, why they're important, and how your knowledge of them will improve your students' lives. But first, I would like to share the story of my own coming out process.

Coming Out To Myself And My Parents

My parents couldn't have been happier about my love for my new school. I'd come home and my mom would ask me about my day. I'd tell her about the rigorous classes and about the friends I'd met. The stories about all my queer friends would occasionally spark concern.

"Sameer, have you thought about hanging out with straight kids too?" she would ask.

I felt that my friends were the nicest, most caring people I knew, and it didn't matter how they identified. Looking back, I know her question came from a place of worry. It's the same concern I've heard many parents express to me throughout my LGBTQ+ advocacy work.

But I didn't share this concern. In fact, because I had so many LGBTQ+ friends, I joined them at our school's Gender & Sexuality Awareness (GSA) club meetings. I didn't identify as queer then, but I was happy to support my theatre squad. I soon became a weekly fixture at GSA meetings.

Right after winter break, I auditioned with an Indian-American theater company based in Northern California called Naatak. The group was putting on a stage reading of *Safe* by Donna Hoke. It's the story of an effeminate gay kid who is mercilessly bullied and eventually commits suicide. I was cast as a conflicted classmate who is kind to the queer boy in private, but is good friends with his tormentor and remains a bystander rather than stopping the harassment. Preparing for the role pushed me to think about my experience being on the receiving end of anti-LGBTQ+ bullying. I strongly related to the main character and his pain after being attacked.

I started thinking more deeply about my own identity. When I was younger, and my bullies would call me 'so gay,' I would wonder if it was true. At night, I would lie sleepless, tossing and turning, trying to understand why I was being teased. Was I gay? I wasn't really ready for the exploration, but my harassers were constantly planting questions and thoughts in my mind that demanded answers. This is one reason why some LGBTQ+ teens seem to know they are queer at what feels like a pretty young age to many straight and cis adults. We are often forced to think about our sexuality because of the expectations of the heteronormative society around us. We are acutely aware that we are different.

When you fit into the mainstream, you don't question or worry about your identity. But I was a boy obsessed with glitter, mermaids, and ball gowns while living in a conservative, predominately South Asian immigrant community. I grew up feeling I was different, and maybe even defective. Despite having lots of queer friends, I was still holding onto old stereotypes about gay people: biases I had developed by watching caricatures of gay men on TV and listening to homophobic jokes from adults. Even my favorite Disney movies routinely turned to the trope of presenting villains as effeminate men. Scar, Jafar, Governor Ratcliffe, and King Candy with their over-the-top flamboyance and femininity were purposefully 'queer-coded' to seem gay. And the sea-witch Ursula from *The Little Mermaid* was based on a real drag queen and legend named Divine. Talk about early brainwashing!

This internalized homophobia was something that took me a while to overcome. Slowly, I started embracing my own truth. At that point, somewhat fearfully, I decided to come out to my parents.

It was on a weekend in February, 2016 that I finally told my mom that I was queer. We were in the middle of an unrelated conversation when I sprung the news on her. She was confused and a little uneasy, but she tried to sound supportive. Still, she bombarded me with well-meaning but deeply personal questions I wasn't expecting.

"Why don't you try dating a girl before you decide anything? Being gay is a really hard path, and I want you to be really sure. This could have consequences for the rest of your life." She ended by saying she loved and accepted me, which gave me the courage to tell my dad.

He, too, had questions. "Why do you need to label yourself? You may change your mind. After all, you're so young."

These questions expressed a total double standard. I wondered what it would look like if straight kids faced the same inquiries. If a straight fourteen-year-old told his parents, "I have a crush on a girl at school," would they reply, "A girl? Honey, isn't it too early to know? Why don't you wait and see if you get a boy crush? Then we'll talk…"

Although my parents comments saddened me, I also knew they loved me no matter what, and would never want to hurt me. Their response was in no way hostile or threatening. Considering the nightmarish coming out stories many teens experience, I'm one of the lucky ones.

About a month after I came out to my mom, she surprised me with a 'coming out' gift basket. Purple is my favorite color, and the basket was overflowing with purple candies, a purple t-shirt, a purple mug, purple stuffed toys, and more. The gift was such an unexpected and caring gesture. My parents told me that after reflecting, they felt sorry for how they had responded to my coming out. Rather than celebrating the strength and courage it took for me to talk to them, they tried to change my mind by questioning me. The gift basket was their way of expressing their apology, but also their pride. I discovered that my mom had been reading the books and articles I had given to her, trying to learn more about the LGBTQ+ community. She confessed that they had helped her recognize why all her initial questions were textbook examples of what not to do when someone comes out to you.

Receiving this gesture of acceptance from my parents made me even more grateful for my lucky circumstances. In the conservative community I grew up in, most of my peers' families would have had a dramatically different coming out response, one that explains why acceptance has such a big impact on LGBTQ+ teen depression and suicide rates.

Identifying Our Biases

My own subconscious stereotypes about the gay community and my parents' initial negative reaction to my coming out are examples of the types of hidden biases we carry without being fully aware. We are products of our environment, and many of the experiences we've had in our lives are out of our control. We are influenced by our families, our communities, our religion and more. The impact of our backgrounds on us can lead to biases we don't know we have. Much of the LGBTQ+ activism I do is rooted simply in bringing awareness to people's misconceptions. Shedding light on areas people haven't paid much attention to is the first step in changing their perspectives.

In the case of anti-LGBTQ+ biases, many otherwise open-minded and compassionate people aren't aware that their beliefs have been influenced by their environments. Here are simple questions to ask yourself as you assess your own point of view:

1. What were your impressions of LGBTQ+ people growing up? How were they represented in your community, on TV, online, and in print?
2. Have you heard a joke that stereotyped or made fun of LGBTQ+ people before? Did you laugh?
3. If you're not LGBTQ+ and someone assumed you were, how would you feel?
4. Throughout your life, what have you heard close friends or family members say about LGBTQ+ people?
5. Do you have family members who are openly LGBTQ+?

6. Imagine a close family member came out to you as LGBTQ+. What if it was your mom, dad, brother, or sister? How would you feel?
7. How would you feel if your child came out to you as LGBTQ+?
8. Is it okay for a middle schooler to come out as LGBTQ+? Or is it too early in your point of view?
9. When you view Gay Pride Parades either in person or on a screen, how do they make you feel?
10. Can you name any historical figure you studied about in school that identified as LGBTQ+?

These questions are intended to point out that our experiences matter. Just as none of us were born racist, none of us were born with anti-LGBTQ+ bias either. Both are learned behaviors. If we have any negative beliefs about the LGBTQ+ community, most likely the past has informed our present beliefs. If we seek to expand our ability to empathize with and understand the challenges of the diverse populations in our school campuses, then self-awareness is essential.

A Generational Shift

There's no way I can generalize the beliefs of every student in every part of the country. However, I can describe the trends I've observed through my own research, and while speaking to students from different cities and states. Easy access to the internet means that from rural to urban areas, young people are consuming and viewing a wide range of content. As I described in the last chapter, after hearing that my peer identified as non-binary during our freshman orientation, I searched online to learn what that meant. The internet contains lots of information on LGBTQ+ identities, and in the current political and social climate, LGBTQ+ issues and queer people are often in the headlines.

So, most young people know a little bit about minority genders and sexualities. While they may have different opinions or beliefs about the community, they are definitely getting exposed to it. Yet, the internet is not always right, and there is a lot of misinformation that can be spread easily on social media. As an adult, you have both the tools and the authority to discern misleading or false content from legitimate information for your students. You can use this book, as well as the resources I share, to clear up potentially harmful information they've discovered on their own.

Sex, Gender Identity, And Sexual Orientation

"What's the big deal?" many people ask when the topic of diverse gender identities and sexual orientations arises. "Why so many letters and identities? Aren't we all just people?"

Thanks to the LGBTQ+ friends I met in high school, I realized why having all these labels is important. Labels help LGBTQ+ people express themselves in a world where their identities have been made fun of, dismissed, or ignored. These labels allow us to communicate who we are, find others with similar identities and attractions, form friendships and even romantic attachments.

This is no different from all the other labels we commonly identify with that give us a sense of self, such as "an Irish Catholic Bostonian Male" or "a Latina with Colombian ancestry" or like my dad "an Indian American immigrant tech industry employee." With that said, the idea of memorizing a series of letters like LGBTQ+ may feel daunting enough for you to think, "I'll never get it right!"

In fact, entire Ph.D. dissertations have been written about the acronym LGBTQ+. Both the letters and their meanings continue to evolve, which explains the + at the end. The good news is I'll keep the information basic, so you can implement what you learn right away. I genuinely believe less is more here, and a high level overview rather than overwhelmingly lengthy descriptions will be more helpful. Although, no one letter is more important than the other, the order helps maintain consistent usage that leads to widespread understanding. With practice, saying LGBTQ+ will roll off the tongue just like saying U.S.A., R.S.V.P., or A.S.A.P.

Let's first make an important distinction. Some of the letters relate to sexual orientation, while others relate to gender identity. In the previous chapter, I explained that sex and gender identity are different. Just as people often mistakenly believe sex and gender are the same, many also think of gender and sexual orientation as identical. But sex and gender identity do not address one's attraction to someone else. That's the role of sexual orientation. Sex $\neq$ Gender Identity $\neq$ Sexual Orientation.

If sex is about your body, and gender is about who you think yourself to be, then sexual orientation is about who you're attracted to. A participant in one of my workshops said she had heard it described as "gender identity is who you go to bed as, and sexual orientation is who you go to bed with!" That got a lot of laughs.

To be more specific, sexual orientation is who we are physically or sexually attracted to. Thus a person's sex and gender identity may have no bearing on that individual's sexual orientation. This is also true for their gender expression, defined by HRC as "the external appearance of one's gender identity, usually expressed through behavior, clothing, haircut or voice, and which may or may not conform to socially defined behaviors and characteristics typically associated with being either masculine or feminine."

A boy may have many markers of female gender expression. He may play with dolls, wear dresses, and paint his nails. As a result, people may assume his sexual orientation is gay. But because gender identity and expression are apart from sexual orientation, this may not be the case. It's harmful to this young person when others make assumptions about him because they do not understand that gender and sexual orientation are two different things. The same applies to masculine presenting girls who are labeled lesbian.

Next, let's look at the abbreviation itself more closely. The first L is for lesbian, the G is for gay, the B is for bisexual, the T is for transgender, and the Q is for queer and/or questioning. The plus sign at the end represents many more gender or sexual orientation identities, reminding us that these are both spectrums.

It is important to note that letters L, G, and B represent sexual orientation. The T represents gender. And the Q represents both. The Human Rights Campaign defines these terms thus:

- **Lesbian:** A woman who is sexually attracted to other women.
- **Gay:** A person who is sexually attracted to members of the same gender.
- **Bisexual:** A person sexually attracted to more than one sex, gender or gender identity though not necessarily simultaneously, in the same way or to the same degree.
- **Transgender:** An umbrella term for people whose gender identity and/or expression is different from cultural expectations based on the sex they were assigned at birth. Being transgender does not imply any specific sexual orientation. Therefore, transgender people may identify as straight, gay, lesbian, bisexual, etc.

GLAAD has a media guide that further clarifies, "people under the transgender umbrella may describe themselves using one or more of a wide variety of terms, including (but not limited to) transgender and non-binary. Always use the term used by the person. Many transgender people are prescribed hormones by their doctors to bring their bodies into alignment with their gender identity. Some undergo surgery as well. But not all transgender people can or will take those steps, and a transgender identity is not dependent upon physical appearance or medical procedures."

Now we reach the final letter! Q is tricky for two reasons. First, it can mean questioning or queer. Second, it can represent gender or sexual orientation or both. For example, questioning may represent people who are unsure or fluid about their gender. But it may also represent people who are unsure or fluid about their sexual orientation.

And then there's 'queer.' Although in the past, queer was an insult toward LGBTQ+ people, many youth of my generation use it as a synonym for LGBTQ+. This is often confusing for teachers who were raised to avoid using the word. If you're unsure whether you should use it or not and don't want to offend your students, stick to LGBTQ+. If you have any openly LGBTQ+ students, asking them their preferred designation in a polite one-on-one conversation may clear up the matter for you. The + refers to additional identities. And if you've ever explored these, you were probably initially surprised at how many there were. Many of us queer youth who have been lucky enough to have resources and support to explore our identities are quite comfortable with the dizzying array of queer identifications. We may not know them all, but we maintain an open mind about them. For illustrative purposes, I'll point out a few:

- **Pansexual:** A sexual orientation that indicates an attraction to a person regardless of that person's sex and gender, or an attraction across all sexes and genders.
- **Intersex:** A gender identity described in Chapter 3 that I wanted to share again, because increasingly I am seeing it used in an expanded acronym LGBTQIA+. Here, I is for intersex and A is for asexual. One of my fellow youth activists Jonathan Leggette once explained to me that there has been a concerted movement to add I to the acronym, because "I stands for Intersex, not Invisible!" This is now a national campaign that they are helping promote to raise awareness for the existence of intersex people within the LGBTQIA community. According to Jonathan and the InterACT Advocates for Intersex Youth (interactadvocates.org) "intersex is an umbrella term that refers to people who have one or more of a range of

variations in sex characteristics that fall outside of traditional conceptions of male or female bodies."

- **Asexual:** A sexual orientation where one does not experience sexual attraction or feel the desire to engage in sexual activity. This identity is not the same as having a sexual dysfunction or choosing to remain celibate. Asexual people may still feel romantic attraction, and choose to enter relationships. The Overview of Sexual Orientations by University of California, Santa Barbara estimates that 1% of the population is asexual.

- **Biromantic:** Romantically attracted to two or more genders. Some people have a romantic orientation that differs from their sexual orientation. For example, an asexual person who doesn't experience sexual attraction can still be attracted romantically to two or more genders, making them biromantic asexual. An asexual person can also experience no romantic attraction, making them aromantic asexual.

You'll notice the letter H for homosexual doesn't appear anywhere in my descriptions or in the LGBTQ+ identification. This is because you'll often see and hear it used to describe LGBTQ+ people in a harmful way. Anti-LGBTQ+ organizations rarely use LGBTQ+. Many of these groups believe people like me have a disease, psychological disorder, or abnormality that can and should be cured. They refer to adults and youth like me as homosexual, which can come across as offensive and demeaning. That's one reason why you should avoid it and use LGBTQ+ instead.

In fact, even well intentioned allies can hurt feelings because of language they use, rather than terms they don't know! Even if you don't understand what all the letters of LGBTQ+ mean, or are up to speed on all the sexual orientations and gender identities covered by the plus sign, it's ok. All you need to do is create an accepting environment around you where LGBTQ+ students (or for that matter colleagues and parents) can feel safe opening up to you. If they choose to come out, let them tell you how they want to be identified. Use the terminology they prefer, and when in doubt ask them what it means and encourage them to let you know if you make mistakes. It's as simple as that. However, to create that comfortable and safe space around you, it is more important not to use language that offends or marginalizes. In this next section I will share common language mistakes I have noticed people make (myself included).

Avoiding 6 Language Mistakes

In 2017, The GLAAD Media Institute was testing out a series of new courses, and I was invited to attend one of them. Ross Murray, who taught that session, went into illuminating detail about how slight variations in language can make a big difference in meaning. Many of the tips I share here are inspired by that class.

1) Don't use the word transgender as a noun. Instead treat it as an adjective. It would not be polite to add an 'a' before the word and say "Sameer is a transgender." Instead use transgender person and transgender people. Never add 'ed' at the end to create the word transgendered: no one is gayed or lesbianed, and neither are they transgendered. Finally avoid words that make being transgender seem like it is a condition. For example, anti-LGBTQ+ groups use words like 'transgenderism' to dehumanize and insult transgender people.

2) Avoid asking transgender people personal questions. Don't ask them about their bodies, surgeries, hormone treatments, or transitioning process. First, respect their privacy and dignity. Second, do not assume all people who identify as transgender want to change their bodies, or have certain physical characteristics.

3) Do not say 'sexual preference' when you may mean 'sexual orientation.' Most queer people do not feel like they have a choice or preference in who they are naturally attracted to.

4) Do not use 'gay community' as an umbrella term. Use more inclusive language like 'LGBTQ+ community' instead. This does a slightly better job of capturing the different gender and sexuality diversities within the queer population.

5) Don't use the term 'homosexual lifestyle.' This implies all LGBTQ+ people are one monolithic group with similar lives. In fact, we make up more than 10% of the population. We include Christians, Muslims, Buddhists, and atheists. We belong to all races and nationalities. We live in big cities, and also on small rural farms. Many of us are military personnel, church pastors, school teachers, or elected officials. There is no 'homosexual lifestyle.'

6) Avoid using the term 'homosexual.' As we discussed, this word is now considered offensive by many due to its association with clinical terminology that was used to label LGBTQ+ people as having an illness, disease, or psychological issue. According to GLAAD, "the notion that being gay, lesbian or bisexual is a psychological disorder was discredited by the American Psychological Association and the American Psychiatric Association in the 1970s."

As an LGBTQ+ teen, I would also suggest 3 other things to avoid, especially if you are a teacher talking to a student who comes out to you:

- You are too young to know!
- This is just a phase, everyone explores when they are young, you'll grow out of it.
- I could tell, it was so obvious.

It is important not to minimize the moment by bringing up a student's age or maturity. It usually takes a significant amount of time, thought, and courage to come out to someone, and a teacher should respond by taking the declaration seriously. Similarly, saying anything that implies you have been speculating about their sexual orientation or gender identity before they were ready to acknowledge it also sends the wrong signal. Instead, just listen casually. Neither minimize what was shared, nor blow it out of proportion. Thank the student for trusting you, signal that you are there to support the student, and encourage them to reach out whenever they need anything. Then move on. Treat the student the same as before, and don't make all conversations about them being queer. This will help normalize things for the student.

CHAPTER FIVE

CREATING INCLUSIVE CLASSROOMS

W e are more than halfway through the book now! Congratulations for taking this journey with me. I would like to do a quick recap of some key things we have learned so far:

- Recognizing and addressing anti-LGBTQ+ bullying and name calling
- Understanding the differences between sex, gender identity, gender expression, and sexual orientation
- Learning about the gender spectrum, transgender identities, and using correct pronouns
- Recognizing hidden biases that we may be unaware of, and learning that there is a generational shift in how we think about gender and sexuality (less binary, more of a continuum)
- Learning what all the letters mean in the acronym LGBTQ+, as well as the history and continued evolution of its use as an umbrella term
- Common language mistakes that can be offensive to the LGBTQ community

Equipped with this knowledge, as well as the resources I have shared throughout the book for additional learning, I believe we have accomplished the most important transformation: that of you as a teacher. Just because of what you know, you will be creating a safe space around you for LGBTQ+ students who I hope will seek you out if they need an adult ally.

Now, I hope you feel excited and ready for the next part of the book: the transformation of your classroom and school. I will be sharing ideas and examples with you of easy things you can do to make your classroom more inclusive and your school safer for LGBTQ+ students. Every school is different, so my ideas are meant to inspire you. You may decide to use none of them, or pick and choose the ones that make sense for you. Be creative, have fun, and adapt the suggestions to fit the needs of your student body.

The Tale Of Two Schools

A typical school morning for me starts with waking up at 5:45 AM. I rush to get ready, eat a quick breakfast and leave home at 6:40 AM for the BART station. I take the 7 AM train and hope there are no delays. If all goes well, I do some homework, take a quick nap, or listen to music. Eventually I jump off the train and dash across the platform to catch another one: a train that gets me to the Rockridge BART station. There I wait in line with other students from my school until our shuttle arrives, eventually getting to class in time for the 8:05 AM morning bell. My return trip is inevitably longer because of shuttle timings and delays, and the trains are usually too crowded for me to find a seat immediately. I share all this because all through elementary and middle school, it took me less than 7 minutes to reach school! Yet I would dread waking up in the morning then, while I cheerfully jump out of bed the moment my alarm goes off now.

A large part of the joy I get from attending high school is about the acceptance I feel. I know I belong there, because in both big and small ways this thought is continuously reinforced by my teachers, who set the tone in their classrooms. After years of being bullied, I don't take an inclusive school climate for granted, and notice all effort that goes into creating a welcoming environment.

There are 4 things I learned from observing my own teachers at The College Preparatory School, as well as by talking to teachers around America. By taking any or all of these 4 steps, you too can make your classroom a place where LGBTQ+ students can thrive.

1. Display Inclusive Signs In Your Classroom

Having a clear, visual signal in your classroom that you are a teacher who supports diversity and inclusion can dramatically change things for the better. I have seen signs with broad messages that welcome not only LGBTQ+ students, but also students from different races, religions, family structures, ability levels, body types, language fluencies, socio-economic brackets etc. Better yet, consider adding a specific sign for your LGBTQ+ students to send a stronger signal that you are an ally and someone they can trust and open up to. Many of my high school classrooms have inclusive stickers from GLSEN that catch attention because of their bold, pride colors and the message: "This is a safe and inclusive space for lesbian, gay, bisexual, and transgender students and their allies."

When I asked a group of LGBTQ+ activists and allies to share their one tip for teachers, adding inclusive classroom signage was the most common response.

- "Teachers can post a sticker on their door of either a rainbow or the official 'safe space' sticker from GLSEN. That way students will know it's an open teacher and safe for them to talk without judgment" - Shelby Carter
- "The first thing that popped in my mind was the safe place signs. Teachers sometimes share or rotate rooms though so seems like it should be portable as well as noticeable. Maybe something like a paperweight? There would also need to be a way to communicate to youth in need the

significance of the marker, maybe a hallway bulletin board?" - Kathie McElhinney

- "GLSEN has great safe space stickers that are a nice symbol that show a teacher is accepting." - Sean Bender-Prouty

GLSEN comes up frequently because they offer safe space stickers, posters, and a toolkit that you can download and print for free on their website: www.glsen.org/safespace. If you prefer professional printing, GLSEN will mail the actual items to you for a nominal fee.

You can also be creative and customize your message to suit the needs of your classroom by making your own posters. Think about having other symbols in your classroom, or wearing wristbands and buttons that demonstrate your support for your LGBTQ+ students (for example in October during LGBT History Month). Sometimes a more subtle approach can also work. If you have posters in your classroom consider having some images that include LGBTQ+ people. For instance, same gender couples holding hands or people celebrating pride. Presenting these images is a powerful way to show your LGBTQ+ students they have a place in society and that you support them.

I know that not all campus cultures are welcoming to LGBTQ+ students. In fact, some campus cultures may be anti-LGBTQ+. If you believe it's too big of a leap to post Safe Space posters or stickers in your classroom, there are subtler ways to demonstrate your support as well. I provided strategies in chapter two. For review, you learned why "Saying gay is not okay" and how to support students who are the target of anti-LGBTQ+ bullying.

2. Include Everyone In the Words You Use

As a teacher you are surrounded by students who listen to and absorb the things you say throughout the day. So use language that includes everyone. On the first day of class ask students to introduce themselves by sharing their preferred name and pronouns. You can start yourself with something like "My preferred name is ___ and I use he/him/his pronouns." Just as my high school teachers did, honor students' preferred pronouns. Some students may prefer sharing their identities with you privately, by email or during a one-on-one conversation. In those cases, understand and respect the students need for privacy and do not out them to others. You can still use their preferred pronouns as a way to signal your acceptance when you are alone.

When referring to your class, avoid saying 'boys and girls' or using other overly gendered language when you can substitute words like 'students' or 'people' or 'class.' Don't make an assumption that all students have two parents that are male and female or 'mom and dad.' Instead use a gender neutral term like parent or parents. Rather than always describing married couples as 'husband and wife,' introduce terms such as partners and spouses. Such language helps your class move away from assuming heteronormativity as the default, and subtly acknowledges that not everyone falls within neat heterosexual paradigms.

Finally, avoid perpetuating gender stereotypes in class, and call out any student who does this as well. For instance, if you hear someone say things like girls aren't good at sports or math, and theatre isn't for boys question these assumptions. Be prepared to bring up examples where the stereotypes have proven inaccurate. Highlight the countless instances of girls who excel in athletics and boys who ignored criticism and went on to become beloved entertainers. Better yet, have your students come up with these examples on their own.

Talk about and present images of people who challenge gender stereotypes. Celebrate male dental hygienists and nurses, and female construction workers and soldiers. In addition, point out how behaviors attributed to sex and gender are cultural as we discussed in Chapter 3.

3. Include Everyone In Your Curriculum

Without adding unnecessary complexity, or creating new materials, find opportunistic ways to mention LGBTQ+ people during your existing lessons. LGBTQ+ people have been deliberately erased from public discourse in a way that makes it really hard for young LGBTQ+ students to see themselves represented. So from math word problems to English essay prompts, include LGBTQ+ people in your classroom instruction. Give them a voice!

For example, if a math word problem features a married couple, consider describing them as a same gender couple. One of my friends and fellow HRC Youth Ambassadors Roddy Biggs suggest that teachers should "talk about LGBTQ+ people's contributions to our society and have a class creed about diversity that mentions LGBTQ+ people."

I love this suggestion. Reflect the diversity in your classroom by including LGBTQ+ people in your curriculum and pointing out their accomplishments and impact in the subject matter you're teaching. 12 LGBTQ+ icons worth mentioning:

- Sir Francis Bacon: He argued for the scientific method, which is the foundation of modern scientific inquiry
- Tennessee Williams: A two time Oscar nominated playwright
- Alan Turing: The mathematician who is considered the father of modern computer science
- Florence Nightingale: Organized the world's first school for nurses
- James Baldwin: An iconic American novelist and playwright
- John Burnside: Invented the teleidoscope
- Andy Warhol: Considered the godfather of the '60s Pop Art movement
- Sally Ride: America's first female astronaut and is a Presidential Medal of Freedom Honoree
- Walt Whitman: An influential poet

- Sara Josephine Baker: A physician who re\ American public healthcare
- Katharine Lee Bates: Wrote the anthem A_ Beautiful
- Leonardo da Vinci, who needs no introduction!

Did you notice that people of color are missing completely from the list above? I didn't until someone pointed it out to me! GLAAD put together a list of black LGBTQ+ heroes like civil rights icon, Bayard Rustin; poet laureate, Audre Lorde; musician, Johnny Mathis; and NBA player, John Amaechi. Visit this site for even more examples: www.glad.org/post/honoring-black-lgbtq-icons/

When covering historical events, be sure to include the role of LGBTQ+ people. For example, the Stonewall Riots marked the start of the LGBTQ+ civil rights movement, and opened the doors for equality for queer and non-queer people alike. During the Holocaust, LGBTQ+ people were subject to extermination alongside their Jewish counterparts. Keep books by LGBTQ+ authors in your classroom, and when providing suggestions for essay, research, or debate topics include LGBTQ+ themes and issues. Some states like California have already taken steps to mandate LGBTQ+ inclusion in curriculum, but this is not the norm across the country.

You can see from the examples I provide, that with a little thought and attention it can be easy to slip in LGBTQ+ representation in existing classroom instruction. If something like this has never been done in your school before, and you are concerned about reactions from parents or other school staff, start small. Try the step that feels safest and least controversial, slowly working your way to creating more inclusivity over time.

4. Take An Intersectional Approach to Inclusion

As defined by the Oxford Dictionary, intersectionality is "the interconnected nature of social categorizations such as race, class, and gender, regarded as creating overlapping and interdependent systems of discrimination or disadvantage." It is an acknowledgment that a student may experience bias, isolation, and marginalization based on different aspects of their identities—compounding the oppression they face and making their situation uniquely difficult.

As a queer, trans, brown person with Muslim heritage, born to immigrant parents I have to deal with homophobia, transphobia, racism, islamophobia, and anti-immigrant bias. Perhaps not everywhere at once—but within the South Asian community someone like me may face anti-LGBTQ+ bias and stigma, while in LGBTQ+ spaces they may experience Islamophobia or racism. This can lead to feelings of being alone and not belonging in any group. Among my high school friends we all have very different types of issues we deal with day to day. Even though we are all LGBTQ+ students, we are not the same! So trying to take a one size fits all approach to inclusion doesn't work.

Yvonna Cazares is a queer woman of color, a dedicated community organizer, and a champion of LGBTQ+ youth in her role working for her city's government. She shares her intersectional experience growing up in Palm Springs in the early 90's:

> *Local leadership was not dominated by LGBTQ people yet and bullying, violence, and harassment was still pervasive in schools in Palm Springs and throughout the Coachella Valley. I remember distinctly being bullied for being poor, being of Mexican descent, and 'acting strange' (which I associate now with being queer). I knew I was different when I was about five years old during my first ballet class at a community center, but because I was cussed out by a White experienced ballet dancer for presumably looking at her in the locker room and because I was 'fat and brown' I asked my mom to never bring me back again. At school, I was teased for playing sports with boys while at the same time*

'slut shamed' so it was often a never-ending battle of balancing how your gender identity and sexual orientation was perceived in order to avoid being socially shamed and or violently harassed in the bathroom. Years later through my professional experience, I've learned that many policies aimed at protecting LGBTQ youth were passed in the early 2000s and take a while to implement. Given this, as a professional working at the intersection of education justice, racial justice, and LGBTQ rights, it was my mission to inform youth of their rights and support teachers and staff in the implementation of these laws in order to make schools safer.

In your conversations with your students, keep in mind that their overlapping identities combine to create uniquely challenging situations for them. To be truly inclusive of LGBTQ+ students, your classroom really has to be a place that embraces ALL kinds of diversity including religious beliefs, political affiliations, physical and mental abilities, language fluencies, socio-economic backgrounds and more. It needs to be a place where someone like our young Yvonna—a poor, brown, chubby, queer person of Mexican descent can thrive.

Change Starts In Your Classroom

Whether you're a teacher at an openly LGBTQ+ affirming school or one hostile to queer students, within your classroom you have immense influence over your students' lives. Seeing a safe space sticker may provide hope to a young person who is struggling at home, at school, or both. The gender inclusive language you use in class may affirm a student's identity just when they need that support the most.

Dr. Ronald Holt is a board-certified psychiatrist and leading expert on LGBTQ happiness and mental health. He has also written an Amazon bestselling book called 'PRIDE: You Can't Heal if You're Hiding From Yourself' accompanied by the 'How to Come Out Safely' video series for LGBTQ+ youth. Dr. Holt and I frequently collaborate on projects, and have presented panels and workshops together on topics related to family acceptance, understanding intersectionality, and the coming out process. His message to teachers is very simple:

There are students in your classroom who may be openly or secretly struggling with their sexual orientation or gender identity. It is therefore always important to create a safe environment in the classroom for all. When students see an accepting teacher, they are more likely to come out to you when they feel ready to do so. An unconditionally accepting classroom can make all the difference. This can be done through placing safe zone stickers in the classroom as well as having an open discussion of acceptance for all, including LGBTQ students.

Teachers are often role models for their students, so how you act and what you say can have a big impact on their development and self-acceptance. Most students come to realize their sexual attraction (or lack thereof) towards others around puberty, which is generally 10-13 years old. Some trans youth come out to their parents as early as 2-5 years old. Therefore, discussing LGBTQ+ issues around middle school should not be considered too early and will actually help those youth who are coming to terms with feelings they did not experience before puberty. I grew up and attended middle and high school in Nebraska at a time when there were no resources as there are now for LGBTQ youth. I wish my teachers had had the knowledge or resources back then to provide a safe classroom environment. I believe I would have had the ability to come out in high school if it felt safer then.

Most of my experience has been lecturing and presenting to college students. I have therefore had the honor and privilege of meeting and interacting with several thousand high school graduates from various demographics. LGBTQ+ youth are at higher risks for mental health issues, suicidal ideations, and substance abuse issues. This in not due to being LGBTQ+ in and of itself, but due to such things as discrimination, rejection, and prejudice against them. Studies have shown LGB youth are up to 4x times more likely to have suicidal ideations compared to their straight peers. Some surveys have shown trans youth to be up to 8x more likely to experience suicidal ideation compared to their cis-peers. Education, acceptance, and exposure to LGBTQ+ issues are key.

My experience is students who come from more rural and conservative school districts tend to be more homophobic and transphobic in their beliefs. It is not that they want to think this way, but more because they were not exposed to, or educated about, LGBTQ+ people. This can be a great disservice to both the student themselves as well as to society. Educating the students about LGBTQ+ issues can be a real eye opener for most and help them assimilate into a more diverse and accepting society. School districts who do not teach about, or acknowledge, LGBTQ+ issues are ill preparing their students for entry into a very diverse society we now live in. I have also experienced those LGBTQ+ students who come from more conservative educational systems suffer from more internalized homophobia and internalized transphobia, which can lead to more mental and physical health distress. Even today, teachers can be fired in Nebraska based on sexual orientation or gender identity. If teachers do not feel safe, we cannot expect them to create a safe environment for their students. It is my hope that one-day laws will protect against being fired for

sexual orientation or gender identity in all 50 states.
- Ronald Holt

I share Dr. Holt's recognition of both the incredible power and the accompanying challenges teachers have in trying to create safe classrooms. Your classroom may be the only welcoming place on a campus that feels lonely or scary to your LGBTQ+ students. Or it may be one of many that embraces diversity and strives to bring out the best in each student. Regardless of where your campus lands on the LGBTQ+ affirming spectrum, your students will benefit when your perspective is open, embracing, and evolving. You don't have to understand everything, or get it a 100% right. The important part is that you express interest in your students' diverse backgrounds, empathy toward the obstacles they face, and respect for their strength, journey, and uniqueness. In the next chapter, you'll learn about how to extend your LGBTQ+ support from the classroom to the campus.

CHAPTER SIX

CREATING INCLUSIVE
SCHOOLS

At the beginning of my sophomore year, I found myself back in my old middle school. I sat waiting for my appointment with Ms. Kim, who had been my counselor during my time at Hopkins Junior High. It had been over a year since I had seen her, and looking around at all the familiar sights and sounds of my former school, I reflected on how much I'd grown since I'd left. I was no longer the same kid, an easy target for bullies to pick on!

After coming out and receiving the support I needed from my parents and school, I finally felt free to be myself and to explore my LGBTQ+ identity. In learning more about myself, I took advantage of the wealth of information available to me: I borrowed books from the library, read news articles, watched documentaries, took courses online, and signed up to become a member of organizations like GLSEN and HRC. It was a time of excitement, but I was also saddened to learn about the history of oppression faced by LGBTQ+ people, and the fact that my experiences with bullying were the norm for most queer students. I couldn't help but feel lucky that things had turned out so well for me. However, I also felt that I had a responsibility to help others still facing the kind of harassment that I had gone through. During the summer after I finished my freshman year, I decided to start a nonprofit called The

Empathy Alliance, with the goal to put an end to the bullying of LGBTQ+ students like me in schools.

Around the same time, I read a *Newsweek* article claiming that Pope Francis said a society that accepts transgender people is "the epoch of sin against God the Creator," and he was upset that "today, in schools they are teaching this to children — to children! — that everyone can choose their gender."

Even though I am not religious, I have admired Pope Francis' message of universal love and acceptance. Unlike past popes, he has also softened the Catholic church's stance towards homosexuality. So the Pope's comments about trans people felt very different from his usual spirit of compassion. As I read article after article about this, I wondered why everything was from a grown-up perspective? I knew it was important to add a youth perspective to the national dialogue.

I drafted an op-ed piece, and sent it to *The Huffington Post*. To my surprise, I received a response from Arianna Huffington herself, with a note that my voice as a teen was extremely valuable. She invited me to become a regular blogger, and prominently featured my article, "Dear Pope, Don't Transgender Children Deserve Your Love Too?" in the online publication, as well as HuffPost's Queer Voices section.

With my permission, my mom shared my article on Facebook making it clear to our entire community and larger family that I was queer and gender nonconforming. Suddenly everywhere I went, I was surrounded by people eager to learn more about a topic that was largely treated as taboo before. I enjoyed the ability to share my newfound knowledge, and came up with creative ways to explain some of the things we have covered in this book around gender identities and sexual orientations.

These experiences gave me confidence and helped me realize that I had something of value to share as an LGBTQ+ teen. One day, I was at Panera Bread when I ran into one of my Hopkins middle school teachers who I had been close to. She had made science fun, and I enjoyed catching up with her. We were discussing 9th grade physics when she noticed my pride t-shirt with unicorns and a rainbow. By this time I was quite comfortable with my identity and came out to her.

"I have a gay sibling too," she said. The news put a big smile on my face.

"How was middle school for you?" she asked.

"To be honest, it wasn't easy," I said. I then highlighted some of the bullying experiences I had faced. Her response at Panera Bread reflected the same kindness she demonstrated in the classroom.

"I think we want to do better at our school," she said. "You should come and share your experience with us so we can make improvements."

I immediately knew that was exactly what I wanted to do! All summer the need to do something about the epidemic of anti-LGBTQ+ bullying had been eating away at me, and the chance to return to my own school and make changes there made sense. I went home and drafted an email to my middle school counselor, Ms. Kim, asking her for a meeting.

The Importance Of An Adult Ally

As I waited in Ms. Kim's office a few weeks later, I wondered what she would think of the new me, and my ideas for bringing change to Hopkins. Ms. Kim greeted me with a big, warm hug, immediately putting me at ease. When I told her that I was queer, she responded very respectfully, making it easy for me to open up. I recounted the bullying I experienced at Hopkins, as well as the lack of any information or education about LGBTQ+ identities. I really believed that lack of awareness was the root cause of bullying, and a little education could change the culture. I then asked if I could introduce to Hopkins some of the strategies and programs that I had benefited from at my high school. Ms. Kim couldn't have been more supportive and receptive to my personal account as well as my pitch. With her on my side, I started gathering resources and recommendations on diversity best practices in schools.

I found the GLSEN safe space stickers and toolkit mentioned in Chapter 5, and passed that information on to Ms. Kim. I also developed and conducted a survey to better understand common issues faced by LGBTQ+ students who come from different middle schools around the Bay Area. The survey titled *LGBTQ+ Initiatives in Middle School* informed participants that I was hoping to "make schools safer and more inclusive for LGBTQ+ students and allies. In the wake of this (2016) election, I think it's more important than ever to start education about diversity at a young age and make schools safe for everyone."

I then presented the results to Ms. Kim in the following email:

Ms. Kim,

I had the opportunity to conduct the survey we discussed. The response was amazing with 42 students participating, and providing data for programs/experiences in almost 24 unique Bay Area middle schools. There were both public and private schools represented. Here are preliminary results:

1) A large majority of students expressed dissatisfaction with their middle school's programs for LGBTQ+ students. 62% of students were slightly or extremely dissatisfied with their middle school's programs to create a safer and more inclusive environment for LGBTQ students (giving scores of 1 or 2, on a 5 point scale). Among LGBTQ+ students, that number rose even higher to 71% being slightly or extremely dissatisfied.

2) A majority of students said they had experienced or witnessed bullying and harassment targeting those perceived to be queer. 52% of total respondents, and 65% of LGBTQ+ students said that either they or someone they knew in school had experience name-calling, bullying, or harassment as a result of actual or perceived gender

identity, or sexual orientation. Interestingly, 44% of non-LGBTQ students had still experienced or witnessed harassment. That is a high number and shows this issue impacts EVERYONE, not just those who are queer.

3) Bay Area middle schools are slowly starting to acknowledge the needs of LGBTQ+ students, but there is still work to be done. 48% of students said that their school did not offer any LGBTQ+ awareness or support initiatives. In schools that did have programs, health/sex-ed was the most common forum for learning about sexual orientation. Only a handful of schools offered all the programs listed: student clubs, assemblies, zero tolerance for harassment, curriculum inclusion, and health education. Both LGBTQ+ students and straight ones expressed pride and satisfaction in these schools.

4) Finally, when asked what their school could have done better; 39% of students expressed a desire for more education about LGBTQ people, integrated in curriculum or offered through schoolwide presentations or discussions. Many students repeated the sentiment that "anything at all" would be great. LGBTQ+ students mainly seemed to seek acceptance and safety. Straight students wanted more education because they felt ill-prepared for the diversity they experienced in high school.

You had suggested that I present these findings to the Hopkins staff and faculty. Would this still be helpful? I have interesting anecdotes, quotes, and program ideas that I think would prove valuable.

Thank you,

Sameer Jha

First I would like to admit that this was a small, informal survey done by a 10th grader. There is a larger scale survey on school climate by GLSEN, and recently HRC also conducted a detailed survey of LGBTQ+ Youth. Both these surveys are national in nature, and more in-depth with numerous questions being answered.

Still, I think it is really useful to get an accurate assessment of your local schools' climate towards LGBTQ+ students through one-on-one conversations, anonymous suggestion boxes, or by creating simple surveys like the one I did. I was very surprised at the results I got for schools in San Francisco Bay Area, which is known for its LGBTQ+ friendly environment. If queer students here weren't receiving the support they needed, I knew in other cities and states with less positive attitudes towards queer people things must be a lot worse. This added to my resolve and I became deeply committed to ensuring that I could make The Empathy Alliance dream for ending anti-LGBTQ+ bullying a reality.

At Hopkins Junior High, Ms. Kim and I were starting at ground zero. It was a school with more than 1,200 students, where LGBTQ+ topics or issues were not represented in student clubs, school assemblies, or class instructions. It was like queer students were invisible to everyone except the bullies. I asked one of my straight ex-classmates from Hopkins this question, "As far as you recall, what LGBTQ+ related topics, historical figures, or health facts were included in the Hopkin's curriculum? Were there any assemblies or classroom discussions that made you more aware or informed about the LGBTQ+ community?"

Her response was simple: "None!" She admits now to wishing she had "learned the differences between gender and sexuality," and feels it would have been beneficial if Hopkins had offered "an LGBTQ+ student club, panels or other events to educate students about the community." And what could the school have done better to make the environment more friendly and inclusive? According to her, "educating students about the LGBTQ+ community. This is not a part of the current curriculum so students mostly learn about it from the Internet, where they can pick up misleading information (leading to stereotyping, harassment, etc...)." This just goes to show that even straight students can benefit from LGBTQ+ education and inclusion.

In the weeks following my first meeting with Ms. Kim, I shared many resources with her, including information about starting GSAs. In my work, I have constantly heard from peers that the presence of a GSA Club can make a tremendous difference in their school experience. Such a club provides support, affirmation, information, and a safe space where students can be themselves. Through our correspondence, Ms. Kim grew increasingly convinced that her school needed and was ready for a GSA, and she was fully supportive of my willingness to kickstart it. She worked tirelessly to clear all the bureaucratic hurdles on my behalf, and on December 21st, 2016, Hopkins had its first GSA meeting during lunch.

In the next section, I'll describe how the first meeting went. You'll also learn how you and your students can work together to start a GSA on your own campus.

Changing A School's Culture

I was eager to make the GSA kickoff at Hopkins a success. To promote the meeting, I designed a flyer and posted it all around campus. In order to attract hungry middle schoolers, I made sure that "FREE PIZZA" appeared prominently. While working on the flyer, I also remember having a debate with my parents about using the term 'Gender & Sexuality Alliance.' They thought the word 'sexuality' was too risqué and could cause other parents to get upset. I compromised by changing the club name to 'Gay Straight Alliance' while in smaller print adding that we would be learning about gender and sexuality. A similar battle ensued over a resource guide I created with common terms and definitions. My mom had me replace numerous words, and also tried to warn me that the principal may not allow me to share the guide with students.

Ms. Kim had another warning. While she was supportive of my efforts to start a GSA, she also tried to make sure I was being realistic.

"Sameer, don't bring a lot of pizza (you don't have to bring any!). There may only be a few students, so don't be too disappointed." Ms. Kim knew the bullying I'd gone through, and she was concerned that any LGBTQ+ students still at Hopkins would be influenced by peer pressure, and would be too fearful or embarrassed to show up.

Finally, the much anticipated day arrived. As we waited for the lunch bell to ring, Ms. Kim and I stood in the room wondering how much pizza we would have left over at the meeting's end. Within the empty room, the first slide of the presentation glowed on screen, displaying the title *Starting Your Gay-Straight Alliance Club*. On one table was a sign-up sheet along with photocopies of the 'terms & definitions' resource guide. Despite my mom's worries, Principal Brown had approved it after a quick review.

Still, I was a little anxious. I noticed that my mom, Ms. Kim, and Principal Brown were all worrying about different things. Clearly I was starting something where the stakes were high, and I did not want to fail.

Then the bell echoed across campus. A few students filed in, receiving their complementary pizza. More students trickled in, and suddenly the pace picked up. Within 5 minutes all the pizza vanished (I had ordered 5 large ones!). Even without the promise of free food, students were lined up outside waiting to take a seat. By the time I started my presentation, 60 students were packed into a room that was at capacity. A teacher hearing about the crowd came by to stand guard at the door because allowing more students in would be a fire code violation. Ms. Kim and I were stunned!

At first the students were quiet, but slowly they seemed to lose their fear and started asking a lot of great questions, even with their peers present. I walked them through the statistics on bullying, and asked if anyone in the room had heard anti-gay slurs being used as an insult. Each and every student raised their hand. I then explained how a Gay Straight Alliance Club can change the school climate: a teacher offered to become the sponsor, and almost ten students raised their hand to sign up to lead such a club. I was thrilled.

The principal approached me afterwards. He expressed his surprise at the high turnout and clear student interest and asked, "What do you need?" Receiving support from the school's highest levels reassured me that the GSA would receive the resources it needed to take root. The full sign-up sheet afterwards showed me that students were willing to bear the responsibilities of taking charge of the club.

Indeed in the two years since, Hopkins has undergone a dramatic transformation thanks to the presence of an active and visible GSA. Every time I go to conduct a workshop, I notice more changes for the better. Where once there was not even a single openly queer student, now courageous teens are able to come out to their peers and teachers. Staff and faculty have started going through Gender Spectrum training, students are no longer divided/organized on the basis of their gender, and at school dances, prom, and during physical education the dress requirements for students have become less restrictive based on outdated gender specific standards. One trans student was immensely proud that they were able to wear a suit to their graduation. Recently some straight Hopkins GSA members who were also part of a girl scout troop decided to do a community service project on anti-LGBTQ+ bullying. As allies, they took to libraries, community centers, and other schools to spread awareness for the need for LGBTQ+ youth acceptance. Finally, when there was an intense debate over updating the health-ed curriculum in Hopkins and other district schools to be more inclusive of gender and sexuality diversities, many teachers showed up to long school board meetings to passionately advocate for the needs of queer students. I could not have been prouder to witness these ripple effects. When I started I felt alone, now I am a small part of a large network of LGBTQ+ champions, and together we are changing not only one school, but all 42! And not just 42 schools, but our entire city. Everyone from the mayor, city council, faith leaders, school board members, and even our congressman have attended educational events I have helped organize.

Change Is Possible If You Believe In It!

Before we dive into the next section which is focused on starting and maintaining a GSA Club, I would like to share some observations from an old Hopkins classmate who recently came out.

"I can't recall a single student who was out while I attended Hopkins, but I knew multiple students who chose to stay closeted. I'm not really sure what the environment was like towards LGBTQ+ students because no one ever really talked about it. It was an unspoken subject. I did not witness someone being bullied because of sexual orientation but I heard kids in the past repeatedly name something as gay

because they didn't like it or it wasn't cool. In high school, there was a huge increase in openness and acceptance of the LGBTQ+ community, which is partially why I think so many students came out much later in their high school career. I think that if Hopkins acknowledged the LGBTQ+ community more openly and educated the students of such topics, Hopkins would be much more inclusive. I don't remember learning even a bit about LGBTQ+ related topics from school. I resorted to the internet and YouTube to understand myself and this community. It would have been great to have LGBTQ+ inclusive sexual education, and unisex bathrooms. Hopkins didn't have a GSA, and if they did have a club for LGBTQ+ students when I attended, it would have made a big difference. Clubs like these can help educate students, especially those who are questioning themselves or unsure how to interpret their feelings. Having a LGBTQ+ club would also promote positivity with the LGBTQ+ community instead of the negative stigma we often find surrounding it.

I would have known that being LGBTQ+ was not something I needed to feel ashamed of."

Hopkins Junior High today is a much different environment. Change started happening because one school counselor was brave enough to partner with her old student (that's me!) to try something new. Change continued to happen because a teacher stepped up to sponsor a GSA club, and a few current students decided to join and lead it. Change did not require a lot of money, time, or effort—yet it rapidly transformed the entire school culture. I hope this story inspires you to also think of ways in which you can bring change to your school.

How To Start A GSA Club

Your school may already have a GSA. If so, quickly skim through the rest of Chapter 6, which is designed to provide help for setting up a new GSA from scratch. Do reach out to your school's GSA leaders and/or the faculty sponsor and ask how you can support them. I am sure they will appreciate your effort to be an ally. However, if your school does not have a GSA, read on.

One of the best ways to ensure your school has a thriving GSA is to help start one, and become its sponsor. Your role and involvement may vary depending on the grade level, amount of student engagement, and overall climate of your school. Eventually a student-led, student-run organization will be most effective, but it may take some time for that to happen. Some teachers choose to partner up and become co-sponsors together to make the process easier.

When thinking about the value of a GSA, Dr. Ronald Holt, a psychiatrist and an expert in LGBTQ+ mental health shares: "Gay Straight Alliances (GSAs) in schools are an important part of keeping the student body safe, educated, and reducing the amount of discrimination and suicidal thoughts in all students. There is a study that was published in January 2014 by the University of British Columbia entitled, *Gay-straight alliances in schools reduce suicide risk for all students*. The study's key findings in schools with gay-straight alliances that were implemented for three or more years showed

- The odds of homophobic discrimination and suicidal thoughts were reduced by more than half among lesbian, gay, bisexual boys and girls compared to schools with no GSA.
- There were also significantly lower odds of sexual orientation discrimination for heterosexual boys and girls.
- Heterosexual boys were half as likely to attempt suicide as those in schools without GSAs."

Clearly the presence of a GSA can have a substantial impact on LGBTQ+ student wellbeing. It is also relatively simple as a cultural change tool. You may need just one sponsoring teacher and, depending on your school's guidelines, one student to form a GSA. You don't have to challenge policies, create new curriculum, or modify facilities to start a GSA (although these things may happen as a result of club member advocacy later on).

Let's review the different roles a GSA can play for LGBTQ+ students:

- **Support:** A GSA can provide a safe space where students come together in a confidential and supportive environment to discuss issues and express themselves. GSA sponsoring faculty should help students create a place that is free of harassment, where differences are respected.

- **Education:** Students can read books, host speakers, and learn together about what it means to identify as gay, lesbian, bisexual, transgender, questioning, and many other identities.

    GSA sponsoring faculty can suggest reading materials, provide speaker lists, and help students navigate school rules/policies. Funding help may be another requirement.

- **Socializing/Fun:** GSAs create a sense of community for LGBTQ+ youth and straight, cisgender allies. They may lessen the sense of isolation that these groups experience. Rainbow parties, a queer prom, and a GSA outing are some ideas, and a sponsoring faculty can serve as a chaperone.

- **Advocacy:** Some clubs choose to focus on change in curriculum, culture, and policies. Club members may choose to advocate for a specific cause, or have a more general list of suggestions. Common issues tend to include things like reducing bullying of those perceived to be different, gender-neutral bathrooms, dress code guidelines, representation of LGBTQ+ role models in classroom lessons, and LGBTQ+ inclusive sex ed.

You can meet with the GSA student leaders to decide on your GSA goals. Often GSAs evolve over time as the needs of the students and the school change, so make sure you have an annual review to update the GSA objectives.

In many ways, a GSA is really no different than any other student club. Follow the school rules and consult the student handbook to ensure you are following proper procedure.

However, there are a few key differences that are worth keeping in mind before launching a GSA:

- **Engage others:** Inform important stakeholders of your plan and get their commitment to support you. This may be your principal, assistant principal, a school counselor, and/or some teachers. When you have the school staff on your side, your club has a higher likelihood of success. You may need to be persuasive, and overcome initial hesitation. Use the statistics and information shared in this book to build your case for why a GSA is valuable. Also bring anecdotal evidence from your experiences with students to demonstrate the need for a GSA.
- **Plan for privacy:** To make LGBTQ+ students comfortable, unlike other clubs a GSA requires a more private meeting location where students can be open and talk freely without fear of being judged. Perhaps a classroom, office, or section of the library can be set aside for weekly GSA meetings.
- **Establish guidelines:** What tone will the student leadership team set when dealing with each other and the GSA members? They may need some training or prep to be effective facilitators of the GSA. Write down some key guidelines around confidentiality, respect, diversity, listening/empathy, etc. For example, "Anything shared in the confidentiality of this space should stay here," or "Assume positive intent and seek to spread knowledge, not shame or ignorance."
- **Define your role clearly:** LGBTQ+ students need extra support. As they meet with each other, they may share problems, confess

emotions, and make decisions (like coming out to parents). Be clear with the GSA leaders and members on how and when you want to be engaged. If a student seems like they are at risk, ask to be informed. Let students know if you are available to talk and be a resource when they are dealing with personal issues. Think about how and when you will consult the school counselor, or any other staff that the school has for dealing with sensitive issues.

According to the American Civil Liberties Union (ACLU), "While school administrators sometimes balk at allowing students to start GSAs, federal law guarantees that students at public high schools have the right to do so. Under the law, there are two types of clubs in public high schools: curricular clubs (those that relate directly to things that are taught in the school, like the Math Club), and non-curricular clubs (those that don't relate directly to things that are taught in the school, such as the Key Club or Chess Club). The federal Equal Access Act says that if a public high school allows students to form any non-curricular clubs at all, then it must allow students to form any non-curricular club they want—and it also has to treat all non-curricular clubs equally."

Chances are you won't meet opposition, and can think about more fun aspects of starting a GSA, like helping students choose the name! A GSA is the most common name for an LGBTQ+ inclusive club. It used to stand for *Gay Straight Alliance* but people realized that the term excluded other sexual orientations like lesbian, bisexual, and asexual as well as those who are transgender and/or questioning. More inclusive names include the *Gender and Sexualities Alliance (same GSA acronym), Queer-Straight Alliance, and Rainbow Club.* If students want to be creative, let them come up with an entirely new name so they can feel a sense of ownership over their own club.

The Kick-Off Meeting

For your GSA kickoff, get the word out ahead of the meeting through assembly announcements, posters, bulletin, and the school newsletter. Make it very clear that the club is not only for LGBTQ+ students but also their allies. Like I did initially, many students feel more comfortable attending GSA meetings as an ally while they are still trying to figure out their own identity. Try to choose a general topic that everyone can relate to, like anti-bullying or diversity so curious students can attend without feeling like they are outing themselves.

If you already have student leaders identified who are interesting in heading the club, great! Introduce the leadership team and have them share why they wanted to start a GSA. Let them present their goals and vision, but then ask attendees for their input and interests. Have a Q&A and let your student leaders answer questions, but be ready to jump in to support them if needed. End with optional sign-ins for those who want to stay involved and get notified of future meetings. Some students will hesitate to put their names on paper. So you may also want to announce a regular meeting time and place, welcoming students to drop in when they feel like it. As everyone gets more comfortable, the GSA will grow in membership and the initially tentative attendees may end up becoming some of your strongest student leaders. Be patient and persistent. Remember, a GSA with even one student will still be creating a shift in your school culture. Finally, consider bringing some print-outs of information that students can take with them: terms and definitions, a description of your GSA and its goals, the school's policy on bullying and the reporting process for incidents, and a confidential LGBTQ hotline.

Suggested GSA Topics & Activities

Let your student leaders choose how they run their GSA meetings. However, if they need some initial inspiration consider the following ideas:

- Conduct anti-bullying workshops and facilitate discussions. The Tyler Clementi Foundation has a simple pledge that students can read and sign. It encourages them to be upstanders rather than bystanders when they witness something wrong. They also have toolkits for elementary, middle and high school: https://tylerclementi.org/pledge/
- Play games to learn about different identities. For instance, in my GSA we play 'Gay Fish' which is based on the popular card matching game 'Go Fish.' We paste different LGBTQ+ terms and definitions on decks of 52 cards, which players match exactly as they would regular cards. It is a fun way to memorize terms and students enjoy seeing their identities represented.
- Do a film screenings. This can either be an after school outing (I recently took my GSA to watch *Love, Simon*) or an in school screening. Frameline Distribution provides dozens of LGBTQ+ themed films for different age groups through their Youth in Motion program for free or at a very reasonable cost.
- Discuss stereotypes about LGBTQ+ people in popular culture and media. Learn about famous LGBTQ+ figures in history who have made immense contributions to society and contrast that with how LGBTQ+ people are portrayed.
- Read an LGBTQ+ themed book together and discuss.
- Plan social events, like a queer prom.

National Calendar

If possible, register your GSA with GLSEN (https://www.glsen.org) and/or the GSA Network (www.gsanetwork.org) to receive resources and support throughout the year. Your GSA can participate in national LGBTQ+ awareness events, and sign up to get posters, t-shirts, stickers and more swag. These national days are also great opportunities to do school wide awareness efforts. Below are a few suggestions from GLSEN's online calendar:

SEPTEMBER
September 10–16 National Suicide Prevention Week
September 15–October 15 Latinx Heritage Month
September 17–23 Bisexual Awareness Week
September 25–29 GLSEN's Ally Week

OCTOBER
ALL Month: Bullying Prevention Month
ALL Month: LGBTQ History Month
October 9 Indigenous People's Day
October 11 National Coming Out Day
October 19 GLAAD's Spirit Day
October 22–28 Asexual Awareness Week
October 26 Intersex Awareness Day

NOVEMBER
ALL Month: National Homeless Youth Awareness
November 14-20 Transgender Awareness Week
November 20 Transgender Day of Remembrance

DECEMBER
December 1 World AIDS Day
December 10 Human Rights Day

JANUARY
January 15 Martin Luther King Jr. Day
January 15–19 GLSEN's No Name-Calling Week

FEBRUARY
ALL Month: Black History Month
February 5-9 National School Counseling Week
February 20 World Day of Social Justice

MARCH
ALL Month! Women's History Month
March 31 Transgender Day of Visibility

APRIL
ALL Month: Gaypril
April 10 National Youth & AIDS Awareness Day
April 27 GLSEN's Day of Silence

MAY

May 17 International Day Against Homophobia, Transphobia, & Biphobia
May 22 Harvey Milk Day

JUNE
ALL Month! LGBTQ Pride Month
June 28 Anniversary of the Stonewall Riots

Ensure the GSA events represent all voices, especially those in minority. You can encourage your student leaders to shape the topics they discuss so they meet the needs of all their community members. Be mindful of those with different abilities—choose accessible classrooms and events. If needed, translate posters & resource materials in different languages. Engage willing GSA members to advocate for and create these materials for themselves and others so they can enjoy a truly inclusive space for everyone.

Be The Change You Want To See On Your Campus

In this book, I have tried to provide basic information and steps that teachers can easily use without needing a lot of time, effort, resources, or help. We have discussed strategies to transform your presence (zero tolerance for anti-LGBTQ+ bullying), transform your classroom (inclusive visuals, language, and instructions), and even transform your campus (by starting a GSA).

The challenges your LGBTQ+ students face today are a matter, literally, of life or death. It's up to those of us that are passionate and capable of improving the lives of queer youth to do whatever we can to make sure young people attend schools that are safe. As a high schooler, I work hard to advocate on behalf of my generation of LGBTQ+ students. But I know that no student movement can thrive without adults like you who are willing to stand by us. In the next chapter, I would like to introduce you to one such adult who has changed herself, her class, and her school community—modeling many of the things I have covered in this book.

CHAPTER SEVEN

PROFILE OF AN
EXTRAORDINARY TEACHER

Ms. Heidel and I met over lunch at HRC's 2017 Time to Thrive conference for educators. We found ourselves on the same table, waiting for a much anticipated keynote speaker to start their address, and struck up a conversation. I remember all the details of our exchange, which left a huge impression on me, even though I cannot recall a word of the keynote! Ms. Heidel is one of the coolest teachers a teen could ever wish for. She has a young, enthusiastic presence that makes you want to smile. However once we started talking, I realized that her easy mannerisms hid a deep rooted passion for being the best teacher possible for her students. I was incredibly moved by her serious desire to do right by her LGBTQ+ students. Ms. Heidel soon became Bridey, as I got to know her better over the next two days. I learned more about her involvement with her school's GSA, as well as her concern that her rural school community lacked the LGBTQ+ resources available in bigger cities. On the last day she invited me to visit her school's GSA in Tahoe (something that is still on my list of things to do!). We stayed in touch and I was honored to become a part of a closed Facebook group run by Bridey for her students: an awesome online safe space for them to share news, discuss issues, and find ways to support each other. I always knew that if I ever got the chance, I would like to share Bridey's story with a larger audience. This book gave me the excuse I was looking for, to showcase someone who I believe has been a true hero to her students. I worked with Bridey over email to interview her and capture her thoughts in her own words. I hope she will inspire you, like she has me.

Interview With Bridey Thelen-Heidel
English Teacher, English Department Chair, and GSA Sponsor at the South Tahoe High School, South Lake Tahoe, California

SAMEER JHA: You are so passionate about helping each and every one of your students thrive both inside and outside the classroom. Can you share what motivates you? How would you describe your teaching philosophy?

BRIDEY THELEN-HEIDEL: My motivation and teaching philosophy stems from wanting to be the teacher I wish I had in school: the teacher who noticed I was having a terrible day; the teacher who complimented my new haircut; the teacher who called on me because she knew I had a great answer but was too afraid to speak up without being prompted. I shake my students' hands each day (a practice taught to me by a wonderful principal, Mike Greenfield), and I know they laugh about the handshake, but I also know they look forward to it because they know they have been seen. It gives me a chance to say hello, to notice the haircut, to ask them about their day, to congratulate them on an accomplishment, and even more simply, just to take a moment to look each child in the eye and say to them, "I see you." I believe we (teachers) get paid to have patience and to be creative with our discipline strategies; therefore, I rarely—if ever—raise my voice in a stern manner. Rather, I choose to do the opposite of what students expect: call home and say something wonderful about a student who was particularly obnoxious; stand on a table to give me a new perspective (Thank you, Mr. Keating!); walk out of my room into the hall and laugh that they think I am angry; or crank up the music and just dance! After all, high school students have already heard every threat or lecture (and learned how to tune us out) so being ironic sometimes changes behavior simply because students don't know how else to react!

SJ: How did discover your calling as a teacher?

BTH: While working as a substitute teacher, my first middle school assignment was teaching a group of at-risk youth—a group I related to because of my own dysfunctional and transient upbringing. Apparently, I connected well with the students: At the end of the day, the class instructional aide, Joy, literally grabbed my face, looked into my eyes, and declared, "You know this is what you MUST do!" My mother had little respect for teachers and reminded me, "Those who can do. Those who can't, teach." Needless to say, being a teacher was never a goal for me; however, something told me to trust Joy's advice. Years later, at Joy's memorial service, I shared this story and thanked her for seeing something in me that I did not because she changed the course of my life, and teaching was absolutely my life's purpose. As I sat down, our friend stood up and announced Joy's final gift to me. On the last day of her life on this earth, Joy wrote a $5000 check to the ALLY Club (the name of our school's Gender and Sexuality Alliance). Her gift is an ongoing ALLY Club scholarship in her name, funds used to take students to a GSA prom each April, money to support our weekly meetings and to fund our various GSA projects.

SJ: What an incredible mentor Joy must have been for you. I am sorry for your loss. Your involvement with the ALLY club was something Joy clearly recognized as significant and I would love to learn more about it. However, before we go there, can you share an early experiences that helped you understand the challenges faced by LGBTQ+ students in schools?

BTH: While teaching at South Tahoe Middle School, I produced an 80's musical adaptation of A Midsummer Night's Dream. One of the lead actors, a twelve-year-old boy named Alex, played Oberon, King of the Fairies. Alex was a wonderfully energetic young man whose flamboyance both attracted and unsettled students and teachers. I watched as he handled this tension with grace and humor—throwing his arms in the air in exasperation and also quietly eyeing those he felt judged him. Although Alex came out to family and friends after a few years, he was not yet out when playing Oberon. Opening night, Alex's father said something to me that hinted he knew his son's sexuality: "Great to meet you, Mr. Boyar." I said, shaking his hand. "You, too, Ms. Heidel. My son has been cast perfectly for this." I questioned him, "Cast perfectly?" Alex's father clarified, "You know, Ms. Heidel, King of the Fairies!" He laughed and smiled proudly. "Oh, yes, that," His suggestion was uncomfortable, but I understood his humor (as he intended) was how he chose to open up about his son. Years later, as Alex planned his coming out, he asked me what I thought they'd say. I told him, "Well, I think your dad will say something like, 'Oh yah, okay. Can you pass the pepper, please?'" Unfortunately for Alex, his coming out was not as smooth with his peers and teachers. No matter the internal anxiety the taunts, jeers, and stares caused, Alex usually reacted with the same grace, humor, and drama he did when he was my Oberon: throwing his hands in the air above his head like a Rockette and breaking in to one of Cher's songs. Prompted by a few of Alex's teachers who asked me about his flamboyance, I asked Alex, "Why do you peacock around campus, calling attention to yourself? His unexpected response: "I do it because then the bullies and homophobes see me and not the three boys behind me who don't want anyone to know they're gay, too." Alex taught me how bravery can become a conscious habit. Just act brave, and you soon will actually feel brave.

SJ: Alex sounds so courageous! I can relate to the challenges he must have faced being a flamboyant, theatre loving boy. Thank you for sharing his story. Returning to Joy's gift of $5000 for the ALLY Club, she clearly recognized how important this club was to you. Can you describe your journey to becoming your school's ALLY Club sponsor?

BTH: Several years into my teaching career—in 2005— a very popular, honor roll student handed me his suicide note and quickly ran out of my classroom. After reading the letter, I immediately called his father and told him that his son was in crisis. I did not, however, share the details of the letter: the sad truth that this young man had been bullied for several years by both students and adults who wanted him to acknowledge he was gay. This young man had not (yet) identified as gay and felt that the pressure to entertain others' opinions was just too overwhelming to bear any longer. Thankfully, both the boy's mother and his father responded with love and unconditional support, and the young man—who came out after he graduated from high school—is living his truth and thriving.

After making sure my student was safe with his parents, I sat with his letter and thought about the sad truth that if this young person—who had friends, enjoyed great academic success, and had an incredible support system—was struggling so profoundly then there must be many others who were as well. I knew I needed to offer them help before some other sweet, young soul lost his or her will to live. I discovered many high schools had gay/straight alliances (later to be called gender/sexuality alliances): safe meeting spaces at school wherein students could find allies and be themselves. I invited Alex—the boy I previously cast as Oberon— to start a GSA with me, and he was thrilled. In 2006, Alex and Jade, a straight ally, started the STHS ALLY Club, and our first meeting boasted over 100 students, staff, and community members!

When we started ALLY, I didn't really consider that might also be helping adults—parents, teachers, community members. I quickly learned that parents needed to learn how to *come out* to their friends and family that they were the proud parent of an LGBT child. Walking that path was always touching, and I was humbled to be allowed in to a family's confidence. It feels a bit strange to say that in this modern world, people still need help voicing their support for their friends, children, and family members; but, they do. A few years ago, our high school was blessed with a new principal. He was an incredibly ambitious and openly supportive ally, and I was thrilled that I didn't have to have "the talk" with him about my ALLY Club. Within a few conversations, he opened up to me about his sister's recent transition from male to female. Beaming, he shared what he knew about the transgender community and how strongly he felt about advocating for our LGBT youth, so I invited him to speak to our ALLY students, and he accepted. Although I knew he was a bit nervous because he was new in his role of principal, I had not idea that this would be the first time in his professional career he would share his sister's story. Sitting in a circle with more than 40 ALLY members, our principal opened up about when his brother became his sister, and the immense pride he felt being her sibling. At the end of his story, his allies clapped, cheered, and surrounded him with hugs and gratitude. What an incredible opportunity those students shared as they supported and applauded their new principal. They shared a close bond for the next three years he was their principal. Opening up about gender and sexuality is still a taboo subject for so many, but these conversations and opportunities to share can heal in unexpected ways.

SJ: Is the ALLY Club something you plan to continue sponsoring and staying involved with? Where do you see this GSA going next?

BTH: Honesty, I look forward to closing the doors of my GSA. I cannot wait until the mere idea of having a GSA is a redundancy in logic: Why would students need a safe space because all spaces are safe? Why would students need to feel supported because they are all living honestly, and the world celebrates them. That is my wish. Until that day, though, I continue to host ALLY meetings every Thursday, at lunch, in B9—as I have since that first incredibly meeting in 2006. Some Thursdays only one student shows up, and some Thursdays the room is packed. No matter who walks through that door or how many, they always know that ALLY exists and welcomes them. Our school has about 1100 students, so the days when we have upwards of 80 students and staff, that is a massive percentage of our student body showing support for our LGBTQIA youth!

SJ: Many studies have shown that starting a GSA can have an enormous influence on the culture of a school. What impact has the ALLY Club had in your school or community?

BTH: Proudly, our local community college started a GSA in our honor: "Friends of ALLY." Then, just two years ago—after years of fighting a middle school principal who felt a GSA unnecessary because, as she said, "Homosexuality is not part of the standards until ninth grade"—she retired, and we started "ALLY, Jr." at our local middle school. I think it's important to note here that I knew the law allowed us to start the GSA, but I didn't want to begin it with a principal who would fight the students and staff at every step—that was not a great start to a club that had a rainbow motif! So, while I continued to ask her and offered my help and advice to any middle school student who needed it, we spent the time organizing and preparing for her retirement. Gratefully, the new principal was our ally and gave us the green light immediately. Like the high school's first ALLY meeting, the middle school greeted over 100 students at their first meeting! So much for the former principal's assertion that middle school students didn't need a GSA. Incredibly, the middle school gender and sexuality alliance group is actually embedded in our students' schedule as an elective—so cool!

SJ: What are some of the most memorable experiences you have had teaching LGBTQ+ students?

BTH: Teaching for twenty years, I've taught kids across the LGBTQIA acronym, but a few stand out because of the lessons they taught me.

Carmela

Several years back, I taught a feisty Latina who loved the ladies! Her uniform was a slicked-back top knot, white tank, sagging jeans, and a massive grin! At school, Carmela was open about her sexuality—to the point that I was always separating her from some other girl's face! Unfortunately, her family's Christian beliefs had zero tolerance for her truth, so when they found out she was a lesbian, they brought in a priest and preacher to explain her fate: eternal damnation. Because she dismissed their warnings, Carmela was sent to a conversion-therapy program. It took several months, but Carmela realized that the only way to get out of the situation was to act *straight*. So she and a boy—who was also there to "straighten up"—pretended to be a couple: a smattering of mascara, hair curled, and talk of the heterosexual love the two now shared compelled Carmela's release. She played it straight for about three months, and I told her I accepted and loved her, no matter how she identified. Although I adored her without condition, it was a painful few months watching her conform for her parents and her church. We all knew she was faking it: I knew, her classmates knew, and she knew. One morning, the most spectacular thing happened! As my senior English class was starting, Carmela threw open the door, and I immediately noticed her topknot was back! Her white tank was back! And—most importantly—her massive grin was back! She stood in the doorway and exalted, "I'M BACK, BITCHES!" The class erupted in applause, "Yah, girl!" "We love you!" "That's awesome!" They'd missed her. I hugged her and asked, "Wonderful to see you, again. Where would you like to sit?" Carmela grinned, scanned the room, and replied, "With the cheerleaders, of course!" Immediately, the cheerleaders grabbed her a chair and made room for her at their table.

Timothy/Samantha

In 2012, my student, Timothy, taught me about two groups that I had little to no experience with: Bronies ("bros" who love My Little Pony) and transgender youth. Timothy adored all things *My Little Pony*—wearing out his Rainbow Dash t-shirt and describing in detail the personalities of each of the animated ponies. Midway through the semester, Timothy told me he was in love with a guy he met online. I hugged him and thanked him for sharing his truth—then warned him about the dangers of online dating! A few weeks later, Timothy approached my desk and told me that he'd discovered something else about himself: "I don't think I'm gay, Ms. Heidel. I think I'm actually female. Does that mean that if I like this boy that I'm actually heterosexual—you know, if I'm really a woman who is in love with a man?" I hugged Timothy again and replied, "I don't think the label matters—unless it does to you. What really matters right now is what you want to be called. What's your name?" Timothy blushed and said coyly, "Samantha. I would like to be called Samantha." We agreed that for now we would only use the name when no one was around, but each time I did, Samantha beamed with pride. I've heard Samantha again identifies as Timothy—at least publicly—and as male. All that matters to me is that this brave human is happy, healthy, and (fingers crossed!) still a Brony!

Rafael

Rafael was a bit of an outcast: stuttering, shoulders slouched, and the bullies favorite target. During his early years in high school, I watched as Rafael tried to speak with more confidence, stand taller, and fight back when he was harassed; however, it didn't work, and

Rafael grew even more sullen, Serendipitously, Rafael attended a drag show, and that experience transformed his entire being! Under the tutelage of the shows' performers, Rafael learned how to lip sync perfectly, choreograph complicated dance routines, and apply makeup flawlessly, He performed in drag for his Senior Project and was a smash hit! He even took the risk of coming to school several times in full makeup, garnering a lot of positive attention—even from some of the bullies who didn't recognize him as Rafael! Interestingly, as Rosa, Rafael lost his stutter, strutted, and faced bullies with a confidence that made them cower.

Tommy's Mom

When we started ALLY, I had little idea of the impact we would have on young people and their families. Tommy's coming out taught me there is a ripple effect to our actions, and although it may not be felt immediately, it's in constant motion—sometimes resulting in a massive wave that crashes into the shore—like Carmela's exuberant return to herself—or a gentle undulation softly rising on the shore—like Tommy's story.

Tommy came to a few ALLY meetings, always sitting in the back, never speaking, and leaving with a quiet, "Thank you, Ms. Heidel, for doing this." I had known Tommy for many years because I was his seventh grade English teacher, and his mother and I both taught at the high school, although I didn't know her well. After about three meetings, Tommy stayed after and confessed he was ready to come out to his family but didn't know how to begin. He did not think his parents would accept his truth, and this made him even more nervous. Instinctually, I assured him, "Tommy, no matter their reaction, just know they love you so much." I advised him to bring a friend when he told his parent—as a safety measure (unfortunately, some parents I knew reacted violently to the news) and also to be another set of eyes because coming out can be quite surreal—an out-of-body experience—and hearing a play-by-play of those minutes can be helpful. I reminded him, "Tommy, keep in mind that you've been thinking about this moment for a very long time, and your parents may not see it coming so have patience with their reaction. If they don't say the exact right thing, give them a minute—or three— to process. Just breathe and wait. It will be okay. I'm very proud of you." To be safe, we discussed his options if things didn't go well, and I told him to call me if he needed anything.

Monday morning, Tommy rushed in to tell me it went better than he could've ever expected, and he was grateful for the advice of having someone else there because he really was out of his body in those minutes.

Over the years, I've been honored with helping dozens of young people through this part of their journey, and while Tommy's reveal was memorable, it was his mother's reaction years later that was the ripple that finally—and softly—reached the shore. She and I never spoke about Tommy coming out: no knowing glances or shared winks. However, about five years later, her youngest son, a freshman, offered to decorate the hallway bulletin boards, including our ALLY Club board. That afternoon, as I admired his bright and beautiful display, his mother walked up and stood next to me. "Hello," I said. She stared at the bulletin board, "Hi." Realizing she was intentionally not making eye contact, we stood appreciating the bulletin board, silently. Then the ripple made it to the shore, and she said softly, "Thank you so much for what you did for my family. You'll never know how much it means to me that you were there for my son." We turned toward each other shared a long-awaited hug.

SJ: How were your actions to make your classroom/school more inclusive towards gender and sexual minorities initially received by others around you?

BTH: In the early years of our GSA, our school struggled in making the leap from tolerance to understanding and appreciating our LGBT youth; in fact, I was asked several times to change the club to a tolerance club that included other marginalized groups. Although I am an advocate for many unheard voices, at the time, I felt strongly (and still do) that our LGBT youth needed their own space to speak honestly about their daily struggles— even just to gossip openly about who they had crushes on; therefore, I started the ALLY Club GSA and followed our mission statement: *The STHS ALLY Club provides a safe space for LGBTQ youth.* One of the key successes to our club is that we constantly remind ourselves that being an ally means we have our own *coming out* to do—letting students, parents, staff, administration, and community members know we support the LGBT community. Although I've been asked many times about being an ally, an instructional aide at my school (who is also a member of a local church that is not fond of our club) asked me a question I'd never been asked before. Stepping into my classroom and making sure no one else was around, Debra asked me (in a hushed voice), "The people at my church believe you promote homosexuality. Do you?" I stopped and thought briefly about the connotation of the word "promote"—because I am an English teacher, after all. Then I laughed and replied, "Well, I see you're wearing a San Francisco Giant's shirt, and I'm assuming you're not on the team, right? But, you think they're great and want everyone to know you feel that way? You'll stand up for them if anyone tells you differently?" She raised her voice and answered enthusiastically, "Yes, I love the Giants!" I said, "Well, then I guess just as you promote a team you aren't really part of, so do I. My answer then is, yes, I do promote homosexuality. I think my gay students are awesome, and I'll defend that to anyone who says otherwise." She looked at me, a bit puzzled that I agreed with her church's fear that I was spreading this worrisome propaganda. As she struggled to search for her rebuttal, I admit I cut her off, "You know what your church really needs to worry about is how much we promote heterosexuality on this campus! Seriously. Have you seen what we do? We invite a bunch of teens to a huge, dark room and play sexually suggestive music for them. The adults feign chaperoning by standing at the edge of the room and hoping they aren't needed. We then send all these wound up, hypersexualized students to the privacy of their cars! I cannot even imagine what happens next, can you? So, you see, it's not the gay students we need to worry about; it's those straight kids. They need our guidance. Tell your church members they are welcome to come chaperone. I think that would be wonderful!" She left my room. To her credit, the following week, that wonderful woman came in and bought an ALLY t-shirt—which she proudly wears every Thursday (along with dozens of educators throughout our school district—from elementary to high school). Debra even stood up to many of her friends from church about the work ALLY does at our school. I love when teachers are still willing to be students.

Keeping in mind that I never want any student to feel as if her or his voice doesn't matter, I am respectful of everyone's political and religious beliefs, even those I vehemently oppose. Our right to speak freely and exercise our politics and religion safely is the most precious gift our constitution gives to us. With that known, I also make sure that my classroom reflects my students: their prized writings, beautiful artwork, and many messages of acceptance for all, including my 4x4 "Born This Way" flag that hangs in my doorway. Students know when they enter my classroom, they are loved—all of them. As teachers, we are challenged by our students' beliefs and wary of their ignorance, but it is our job to hear them, value their beliefs, and hopefully make a connection that allows us to educate them. As Oprah suggests, "When we know better, we do better"; years ago I discontinued separating groups by gender, learned how to use they as a singular pronoun (yes, even an English teacher can do this! In fact, my entire English department agreed that using they as a singular pronoun was an easy change— especially when children's lives could be the cost of holding to some silly grammar rule). As a teacher of Shakespeare, we have multiple opportunities to play "Dress Up" in my class, and I always find it wonderful to see how many boys rush to the costume box and grab gorgeous gowns—sometimes fighting the girls for them! Giving students the freedom to express themselves in a variety of ways creates opportunity for trust in a classroom setting. In terms of our campus climate, we have worked hard over the years to bring groups of students together who might not otherwise: campus clean up with the Active Christian Teens, "Clubbin' Night" at the local ice rink, a schoolwide t-shirt campaign combatting hateful language, an annual formal wear exchange for any student who cannot afford a prom dress or suit, staff appreciation days wherein we gift staff with rainbow cupcakes, LGBT-themed movies, and positive "vandalism"—using rainbow colored chalk to write encouraging words all over the school's sidewalks!

SJ: I love the idea of positive vandalism with chalk! Your school sounds very inclusive. How would you rate it in terms of its programs for LGBTQ+ students? How has the climate evolved over the time you have been a teacher?

BTH: Until I attended Human Rights Campaign's "Time to Thrive" conference in Washington, D.C. last year, I didn't realize how incredibly progressive my little, mountain town's school district is—and has been since the inception of the ALLY Club in 2006. At the HRC conference, I was shocked to meet teachers, counselors, and even school nurses who had to pay their own way to the conference—and who were directed not to speak about what they learned at the conference. Many of these educators were from California, and this added to my disbelief because California is, well, California! Our school district and local teachers' union have both been incredibly supportive, paying for me and other staff to attend multiple CTA and NEA LGBT issues' conferences as well as HRC's "Time to Thrive" conferences. I've also been invited to train staff about a variety of LGBT youth concerns. Although I am not naive enough to suspect our work is done, I am also incredibly proud of our school district and appreciate all the freedom I've been given in my efforts to protect LGBT youth and their families. We still hear the occasional derogatory slur and have to contend with the homophobia and transphobia perpetuated by our current administration; however, when I see the ALLY Club celebrated in our local news and hear the accolades across our community, I am emboldened to continue on and to speak even louder for those who have yet to find their voices.

If ever there were a time and place to brag about our high school's inclusive and supportive climate it is now, so I'll share how far we've come since starting ALLY in 2006. In 2014, our school crowned two young men as Homecoming Royalty: Dominique as King, and Kyle as Queen! The ASB offered to create a new title around the ceremony, but Kyle was excited to be Queen—and about his sash and crown. The night was incredible—Friday Night Lights with a massive showing by our community for our Homecoming game. I was honored to drive Dominique around the field, and as we looked at the crowd, I said to him, "I hope you are very proud of yourself and your school. I'm sorry your mom isn't here, and that you didn't tell her about this, but if you win, she'll read it in the paper so get ready." Dominique has a gorgeous, Colgate smile, and he said, "This is amazing. She'll be okay with it." As we rounded the final corner before the announcement that he'd won, the crowd erupted when they saw him.

After he and Kyle were crowned and sashed and selfies were taken, I walked up the sidewalk chatting with friends about the history that these boys created. A friend of mine pulled me aside and said, "Yah, this is fine and all, but what's their agenda? I mean, why did they do this? Are they trying to prove something?" I laughed out loud because I knew MANY of us had an agenda that night, and many of us DID have something to prove; ironically, these two boys were just as popular, attractive, and conceited as anyone else running who ever ran for Homecoming royalty in Any School, USA. They just wanted to win. And, just like other high school couples who get together to win votes, they did too. Although they remain friends to this day, they broke up almost immediately after their win.

What I find to be totally awesome about all this is that is normalizes the high school experience for LGBT youth: not everything has a political undercurrent, and sometimes the gay kid just wants to be popular and feel pretty. That same year, the student body elected an "out" lesbian as Prom Queen! Oh, and the next year, too! I think we are going to survive this administration!

There was one barrier I only learned existed just as it was breaking itself down. Unbeknownst to me, our superintendent was not much of a fan of ALLY. To his credit, ALLY existed more than ten years before I learned of his feelings. These clubs are protected by federal law, so forming the club was not an obstacle, and I heard he protected our right to exist many times over the years. He brought down his own walls in 2014. I was running a silly *Facebook* campaign to meet my favorite band of all time, Duran Duran, and over 1500 people joined me in sending messages to get me to the *Ellen* show to meet the band when they performed. In the days leading up to their visit to her show, I received a call offering me VIP tickets to her show! My campaign had worked, and I heard that I might get to meet her and the band! Although there were no guarantees, I was still thrilled to teach my students that perseverance and setting goals—no matter how ridiculous they seemed to others—was paramount in life. My rural community celebrated with me—even featuring me on a local news program. I then heard rumor that the *Ellen* staff knew about the ALLY Club and were interested in hearing about our work, so I set to getting information to them about the club. Very quickly, my focus turned from meeting Simon LeBon to being even more excited to tell Ellen about our amazing ALLIES (still MUST meet Simon LeBon!) Cue the superintendent: He heard the buzz about the club and came to visit us. As he walked in to our weekly scheduled meeting, he greeted me warmly but didn't seem to notice the size of the group—roughly 80 students and staff on a campus of 1100. As he turned, his eyes widened, he took my hand, and I watched tears form in his eyes. He paused and then said to me, "I had no idea this was what was happening here. Just incredible." He made some other poignant comments, but the fact that he was so touched meant everything to me and to the allies. (In case you're wondering about the show, my friend and I were treated to VIP seating but did not get the chance to meet either the band or Ellen, so I'll probably start a new campaign soon!)

SJ: Good luck with your new campaign! Ellen will love you when she meets you. Like your superintendent, there are still so many teachers and school administrators who wonder why it is important to give special attention to LGBTQ+ students? What would you say to them?

BTH: It only takes one look at the devastating statistics the CDC, GLSEN, HRC, and other groups have compiled around the lives and deaths of LGBTQIA youth to see the time is now for us to step in: wait one day, and another child takes his life; stop to consider the risks, and another transgender woman is murdered; wait to see if our vote counts, and an entire administration strips away the rights generations have fought to win. Our discomfort is not worth the life of a child. Our concern that we might not say the right thing, use the right pronoun, or offend someone's identity hinders us long enough that we are in the situation we are—basic human rights denied, children facing judges fighting for their right to use the bathroom at school, and a generation of LGBT youth seeing the rug LGBT pioneers weaved for them is now being pulled out and used to suffocate them.

At 46, I grew up with a generation who felt like our teachers didn't care. We were part of an assembly line who sat in rows, listened without thinking critically, and even endured corporal punishment during our young lives; thankfully, the old guard has retired and I really believe this generation of educators gets it. We all want to be the teacher who changes lives—who affects positively the way a young person views themselves in the world. Many of my peers are Gen X'ers who fought hard to be agents of change:

showing up to rallies, participating in union strikes, standing up to school boards, and questioning authority (thank you, tenure!). We have it in us to be the safe spaces for our LGBT youth, to be *that* teacher who sees something in that child they cannot yet believe, and to convince this fragile population that it DOES actually get better.

SJ: What advice do you have for teachers wanting to create a safer and more accepting environment for LGBTQ+ students in their schools?

BTH: First, create a GSA—Most importantly, protections exist within the law, so it's not a matter of asking to create a gender and sexuality alliance but just doing it. Again, looking at the statistics, schools with a GSA have a significant impact on the health and safety of not only the LGBT students, but all students and staff. Look to GLSEN or GSA Network for ideas about how to have an amazing GSA and get started today! These organizations offer free posters to hang in the hallways and classrooms. Putting up a "Safe Space" poster in every classroom, office, and student space is crucial to getting the word out and letting students know they are valued and protected.

 Second, train staff—I truly believe we want to do better, so any training specific to the LGBT population is key to helping staff understand their role—whether it's pronoun use, putting a stop to homophobic and transphobic language, or how to create a safe space in a classroom—teachers want to help.

 Third, be the change—This cannot be understated. Gandhi said it, and it holds true that we must "be the change we wish to see in the world." Come out as an ally. Share with staff and students that you have LGBT friends and family members. Provide opportunity for those conversations. Opening up about your story gives permission for others to do the same. While there are so many other ways to create a safer and more accepting climate for our LGBT youth, the key is that each school begins to recognize its own set of issues. Maybe the campus climate is positive but lacks gender neutral bathrooms; maybe there are teachers who are creating gender-specific groups in their classrooms because they don't know other ways to create groups; maybe there are young advocates on campus looking for an adult to advise their GSA, but they don't know you are their ally. Taking a close look at the campus and students is the first step to knowing what is needed and where to begin.

CHAPTER EIGHT

CONCLUSION

W hen I started this book, I envisioned a simple teacher's guide with some tips that would take me a month to create. However, once I started writing, I realized that this book should not just be a list of to-dos or suggestions—something easily available with a quick Google search. I felt compelled to share my story in order to vividly illustrate and persuasively explain all the things I think are important for teachers to know. One month turned into one year, and a few tips turned into a 110 page book!

This period of my life has also been incredibly rewarding and healing. So, I hope to end this book with all the positive things that have happened to a kid who was once thrown a jar of tarantulas at, pushed around on the playground, covered in mud by his fellow scouts, and stabbed with a sharp pencil by his friend—all for the crime of being too feminine.

In 2016, I came out to my parents, my high school, and my South Asian community. I started The Empathy Alliance, penned an open letter to the Pope defending trans children, and returned to my old middle school to initiate LGBTQ+ inclusive programs and a GSA. Since then I have worked with local and national organizations like HRC, the Tyler Clementi Foundation, GLSEN, Trikone, Frameline, GLAAD, and GSA Network gaining knowledge and resources as well as some core beliefs:

1) There is a lot of hard work that still needs to be done for LGBTQ+ equality.

2) I, and every single queer young person, have something important to contribute to these efforts, and can make a difference that matters.

3) I am not alone in this fight. I rest on the shoulders of countless brave activists who have contributed their lives to the cause. In addition, dozens of organizations (that together have millions of members and decades of experience) are willing to help eradicate anti-LGBTQ+ bullying from schools.

4) Supportive educators are the most important part of creating safe and inclusive schools. They make or break the campus climate, lend an ear or give a voice to marginalized students, and most importantly, they teach kindness and equity in the classroom alongside history or math. This conviction is behind my unwavering focus on enlisting teachers as LGBTQ+ allies for their students. I measure the success of The Empathy Alliance, and its progress against our cause, by thinking of the number of teachers we have reached with our message, training, and tools. By empowering one teacher, I know we can change the school experience of hundreds of students.

Our teachers are this nation's unsung heroes: shaping, improving, and even saving young lives every day. This book is an invitation, it is asking you to become an ally. I hope you will consider saying yes! The LGBTQ+ teens in your sphere may not have any other adults in their life that they can turn to. Let them know through your actions that their life is worth living, that their future is bright, and that they don't have to fight all their battles alone. Thank you so much for reading this book!

About Sameer Jha & The Em
Alliance

After being bullied throughout elementary and middle school for being too feminine, Sameer founded The Empathy Alliance at age 14 to make schools safer for LGBTQ+ youth.

Sameer started by doing research on the school climate in 24 Bay Area schools and was distressed to learn that a vast majority of queer students were subjected to name calling and bullying based on their gender identity and sexual orientation. Schools lacked programs to support LGBTQ+ students' needs, and teachers were either ignoring or contributing to the harassment. Determined to make a change, Sameer started with his old middle school where the term 'gay' was only ever used as an insult, no initiatives existed to specifically protect LGBTQ+ students, and LGBTQ+ topics were not covered in the curriculum. Sameer was able to engage the counselor, principal, and many of the teachers and student leaders in his vision to transform the school. Together, they created the first GSA club in school history, added safe space stickers to classrooms, stocked the library with queer friendly books, and encouraged all youth serving adults to take Gender Spectrum training. Sameer's efforts soon expanded to include the entire school district serving over 42 schools & 35,000 students.

To scale faster, The Empathy Alliance decided to focus on 'educating the educators.' A nonprofit that started with one school in one city has grown into a national entity that has reached over one million people across America with a message of love and empathy. Sameer educates on LGBTQ+ topics through keynotes, workshops, op-eds, radio shows, panels, and events throughout the year. He has also collaborated on special LGBTQ+ projects with numerous organizations like Gender Spectrum, ACLU, GLAAD, and Frameline Films. He is now distilling his learnings into a book for teachers to help them create more inclusive classrooms.

Awards & Recognition

For his work with The Empathy Alliance, Sameer was honored as the 2017 Youth Grand Marshal for Oakland Pride, recognized as a 2018 Local Hero by Senator Bob Wieckowski, and awarded a Congressional Silver Medal. Sameer has been featured in publications like The New York Times, NPR, MTV News, The New York Magazine, and Mercury News.

Sameer is a Youth Ambassador for HRC, sits on the National Student Council for GLSEN, and also holds leadership roles within the Tyler Clementi Foundation, Trikone, and GSA Network. He serves on the Mayor of Oakland's LGBTQ Task Force, and received a proclamation from the Mayor of Fremont for spearheading the 1st City of Fremont Pride Celebration in history. Sameer has been named one of the top 10 trans youth activists of color in America, and was featured as Logo TV's Young Leader for 2018. He recently made a 30 under 30 list for international activists that included change-makers like Malala. Sameer's dream is to create an inclusive world where all students feel comfortable being who they are in school—so a need for The Empathy Alliance no longer exists.

Acknowledgements

I would like to thank all the people who accepted me when I came out, supported my efforts to end bullying in schools, trained me to become a better activist, and believed in my dream to author this book. I have been mentored by numerous people and listing all their names would possibly fill an entire book of its own. However, I do want to mention those who have been critical to the creation of this guide. I believe that taking the time to express my gratitude to these adults is important, because I have had the great fortune to benefit from their love and acceptance when so many of my peers face rejection instead. Unfortunately, adult support of LGBTQ+ teens is not something that can be taken for granted. When it happens, it deserves to be spotlighted. The people below are all my heroes and I will be indebted to them forever.

First, my parents who have always been my biggest champions and have given me the unconditional love that I hope every child gets from their family regardless of their gender identity or sexual orientation. They were my first teachers! My grandparents (Arif & Malika Hussain, and Krishna & Manorma Jha) had an incredible influence on me during my childhood years. My two supportive aunts, Ambereen Khala and Naqiya Khala, spent hours going through the final draft to provide valuable editing. Lawrence Ineno, my editor, helped me immensely in creating an outline of this book. From brainstorming anecdotes, designing the book cover, and advising on the publishing process: I am really grateful for his knowledge and support.

I have been very lucky to have had wonderful teachers in all the schools I have attended: Stratford, Learning Bee, Gomes, Mission San Jose Elementary, Hopkins Junior High, and The College Preparatory School. This book is dedicated to all my teachers. I am particularly thankful to Dr. David Robinson and Ms. Julie Anderson for helping me become a more competent writer.

I got my start as an activist at The College Preparatory School by working with my GSA, my awesome peers from the class of 2019 (the coolest cohort ever!), our Director of Inclusion & Equity Jeremiah Jackson, and my GSA sponsor Amy Breed. I love my GSA leadership: Simon, Maddie, and Carson have been the best team one could ever wish for. I am also grateful to our Head of School Monique DeVane, Dean Chabon, Dean Kojan, Martin Bonilla, Kate Kordich, and Lisie Harlow who together with an incredible staff and faculty have helped create a truly unique culture of acceptance. My high school has been a magical place that I will be sad to depart when I graduate later this year.

I have worked extensively with my old middle school where Ms. Amalia Kim, Principal Brown, Mr. Fernainy, Ms. Moore, Ms. Alexander, Ms. Perez, and others supported my efforts to introduce LGBTQ+ inclusive initiatives. A school does not exist in a vacuum but rather in a larger ecosystem—in this case the Fremont Unified School District and the entire City of Fremont. My efforts to impact change in FUSD and Fremont have been the most transformational personal experience because it brought me closer to other LGBTQ+ community members, activists, and allies who I would like to thank (I apologize if I missed anyone): Michele Berke, Sarah Jane Hyde, Monique Manjarrez, Dianne Jones, Laurie Manuel, Brian Davis, Sonia Khan, Beth Hoffman, Martha Kreeger, Linda Dewlaney, Harshita Gupta, Anirvan Chatterjee, Marsha Squires, Shalini Dayal, Ann Crosbie, and all the members of Save Fremont Sex Ed, SAVE, Compassionate Fremont, City Council & Mayor's Office, Fremont Main Library, Town Fair Plaza, Fremont Parks & Recreations, and the Fremont Unified School District.

I have also found mentors within numerous organizations who I am incredibly grateful to: Dr. Vincent Pompei, Tate Benson, Sula Malina, Aldo Gallardo, Mayor Libby Schaaf, Mohammed Shaik Ali, Jason Cianciotto, Ross Murray, Peter Cruz, Rexy Amaral, and Congressman Ro Khanna. They have inspired me to be the best activist I can be. My fellow ambassadors and council members from the Human Rights Campaign, GLSEN, The Tyler Clementi Foundation, and The GSA Network blow me away with their dedication and bravery. Within the South Asian community I have received immense support from the Rewire Community Team (Shailaja Dixit, Yamini Dixit, Roohi Agarwal, and Anjali Rao) and the world's oldest South Asian LGBTQ+ group, Trikone.

A big shout out to Bridey Heidel for responding to my request for a teacher's perspective by writing the entire Chapter 7 of this book! Other amazing contributors include Laurin Mayeno, Dr. Ronald Holt, Yvonna Cazares, and my old classmates from Hopkins Junior High.

A project like this inevitably requires funding. I am deeply indebted to all the donors, some complete strangers to me, who believed in a 16-year-old's vision enough to give generous donations: Kimberly Mooney, Lynn Mancuso, Jason Cianciotto, Ed Terpening, Cecily Smith, Marina Braynon, Erin Ouellette, Lisa Daniels, K.C. Washington, Ashley Mathai, Jennifer Elliott, Peter Cruz V, Joy Lai, Ed Burns, Shavaun Tucker, Sabrina Hussain, Vicki Haber, Nathan Pearson, Mamta Narain, Sara Quinn, Sarah Hyde, Aldo Gallardo, Ross Parish, Brian Davis, Alberto Fassioli, Andrew Chou, Calvin Lin, Sonali Bhushan, Karen Granberg, Archana, Ronald Holt, Eric Selk, Debjani Dutta, Rebecca Schear, Monisha Mathrani, Hrishikesh Sathawane, Dee Miner, Laurie Manuel, Shailaja Dixit, as well as several anonymous benefactors. Thank you also to The Bay Area Reporter and Alex Madison for covering my GoFundMe campaign twice to encourage donations.

Finally, I want to thank all the teachers who are taking the time to read this book because they are concerned about their students' wellbeing. Teachers like you helped me become capable and confident enough to write this book. You are truly making a difference, and saving lives, because you care.

CPSIA information can be obtained
at www.ICGtesting.com
Printed in the USA
LVHW051535240919
632124LV00002B/410/P